SHAYTAN

BY SULTAN–UL–WAIZEEN
MAULANA ABUL NOOR
MUHAMMAD BASHIR

TRANSLATED BY
SHAHID HUSSAIN

*'O believers! Enter into Islam completely
and do not follow the footsteps of Shaytan.
Indeed he is to you a clear enemy.'*

(2:208)

ISBN 978-0-9571096-4-3

First Edition, 2019

Abul Noor Publications

Leicester, UK

publications@abulnoor.com

Design, printed & bound in the UK by OUTSTANDING

Cover calligraphy by OUTSTANDING

بِسْمِ اللَّهِ الرَّحْمَٰنِ الرَّحِيمِ

اللَّهُ لَا إِلَٰهَ إِلَّا هُوَ الْحَيُّ الْقَيُّومُ ۚ لَا تَأْخُذُهُ

سِنَةٌ وَلَا نَوْمٌ ۚ لَّهُ مَا فِي السَّمَاوَاتِ وَمَا فِي

الْأَرْضِ ۗ مَن ذَا الَّذِي يَشْفَعُ عِندَهُ

إِلَّا بِإِذْنِهِ ۚ يَعْلَمُ مَا بَيْنَ أَيْدِيهِمْ وَمَا خَلْفَهُمْ ۖ

وَلَا يُحِيطُونَ بِشَيْءٍ مِّنْ عِلْمِهِ إِلَّا بِمَا شَاءَ ۚ

وَسِعَ كُرْسِيُّهُ السَّمَاوَاتِ وَالْأَرْضَ ۖ

وَلَا يَئُودُهُ حِفْظُهُمَا ۚ وَهُوَ الْعَلِيُّ الْعَظِيمُ

Contents

Foreword

I once said to my respected father that the series of 'True Stories' had been very successful and beneficial for many people. I expressed my thoughts to him that where he has written a series of stories on the "callers towards Allah," he should also pay attention towards the "caller towards evil," namely Shaytan. The "callers towards Allah" the prophets of Allah, the noble Companions, the Ahl al-Bayt and the Awliya Allah enhance our faith and belief and give us a sense of piety to do good things. By highlighting the deception, trickery, lies and schemes of Shaytan, it would give everyone the ability to avoid his ruined path and to gain admonition from it. Alhamdulillah! My respected father Hazrat Sultanul Wa'izeen accepted my request and it is with great honour and happiness that I now present this book to you.

Sahibzada Allama Ata Al Mustafa Jameel
Son of Maulana Abul Noor Muhammad Bashir

Introduction

Why was Shaytan created?

Allah is the wise Creator. No creation of His is made without some reason and wisdom behind it. Whatever Allah has created it has been made with wisdom. Whenever we see something we should say:

'O our Lord! You have not made this in vain!'

Imam al-Ghazali (may Allah have mercy on him) narrates a story in *Kimiya al-Sa'adat* (Alchemy of Happiness) that one day Sayyidina Musa ﷺ was standing on a rooftop when he saw a lizard. He spoke to Allah and asked him why He had made the lizard? Allah responded: "O My Kaleem! The lizard just before you spoke asked me: "O Allah! Why did you create Musa?" Allah then said: "O my Kaleem! Whatever I have made, it has a purpose and wisdom behind it."

It is true that everything is known and recognised by its opposite. For instance, sweetness can only be known if one knows what bitterness is. Good health can only be appreciated if one knows what sickness is. Nice smells and fragrance can be known and liked only and only if one knows what bad and distasteful odours are like. A wrestler can know his strength and courage only when another wrestler comes before him and wrestles. A wrestler can only be called a wrestler if he tussles with someone. If no one comes and wrestles him and challenges him then how can we call him a wrestler? It is necessary that there is someone to challenge the person so that his strength and courage can be known.

For Sayyiduna Musa ﷺ and his miracles to become

known, an enemy and rejecter of the truth – who would oppose and challenge him – was needed. Amongst them is his staff turning into a snake and eating up all the false snakes of the Pharaoh's magicians. The reason for all the miracles of Sayyiduna Musa ﷺ was the presence of his enemy the Pharaoh. If the Pharaoh did not exist then there would have been no need for the miracles. For Sayyiduna Musa ﷺ and his miracles to become known, an enemy and rejecter of the truth was needed who would oppose and challenge him. The challenge posed by Pharaoh to Musa ﷺ led him to display his numerous miracles. Hence Allah created the Pharaoh. The Pharaoh opposed and rejected Musa that in turn led Musa to do miracles which helped defeat the Pharaoh.

The miracles of Sayyiduna Ibrahim ﷺ are also well known. He was thrown into a huge fire, which was cooled down by Allah's command and was turned into a garden. Ibrahim ﷺ rejected Nimrod's beliefs. Nimrod ordered a fire to be lit so that Ibrahim ﷺ could be punished for his denial. But the real denier was Nimrod. Had it not been for Nimrod then the miracle of the cooling of the fire would have not materialised.

Like this, many of the miracles of the final Prophet Sayyiduna Muhammad ﷺ were the result of Abu Jahl. The splitting of the moon, the pebbles reading the Kalima, trees and stones presenting themselves to the Prophet by offering salutations upon him were all the result of Abu Jahl's rejection of the truth. The greater Abu Jahl's rejection, the greater the miracle the Prophet showed. Hence Abu Jahl was not created in vain.

One Friday, I was giving a speech about the blessed saliva of the Holy Prophet ﷺ when I narrated the following Hadith. In the battle of Uhud, Qatada ﷺ was struck in the eye by an arrow. He came to the Prophet for help. The Prophet helped him by placing his blessed saliva on his eye. The eye that was injured was now more beautiful than the other. A person in the crowd stood up and said he rejected it claiming that no such event like this took place. After Friday prayers I began to read up on some books of Hadith and did some research on the matter. The result of the research was that I found even more narrations about the Prophet's blessed saliva and its healing qualities. The following Friday I made public my research and I told that rejecter that you deny one narration when in actual fact there are dozens of narration's that testify to the miraculous qualities of the Prophet's saliva. After quoting all the Hadith I then thanked him. I did this because if he did not reject what I said then I would not have gone and researched the matter further and discovered more Prophetic narrations which prove the curative qualities of our Master Prophet Muhammad ﷺ. So now I can quote several Ahadith about the Prophets blessed saliva rather than the one I had before!

For every miracle and quality of our Prophet there is at least one rejecter of it. An example of this is the issue of the finality of Prophethood. The finality of Prophethood or *Khatme-Nabuwwat* is amongst the miracles and attributes of the Holy Prophet. There are verses of the

Holy Qur'an and countless Prophetic narrations which state unequivocally the finality of Prophethood with Sayyiduna Muhammad ﷺ. But there had to be a rejecter of this fact otherwise there would have been no need for such verses and narrations. If there was no rejecter of the finality of Prophethood then the verses and narrations would have been futile and would not have been read and publicised. Hence rejecters of the finality of Prophethood are also necessary so that the status of the Holy Prophet ﷺ being the final Prophet could be known.

Similarly there are those people who reject and deny the Holy Prophet's knowledge authority, dominion and other qualities, attributes and specialities. When in actual fact there are numerous verses in the Holy Qur'an and Prophetic narrations that support the fact that the Prophet has special knowledge and authority and special qualities and attributes given to him by Allah Almighty. One of the reasons why these facts are stated in the Qur'an and Ahadith is to respond to the rejecters of the Truth.

Sayyiduna Imam Hussain's ﷺ patience, thanks, resolution and perseverance would not have been known if there was no Yazid to oppose him. For the status and honour of Imam Hussain to sparkle, a Yazid was needed. If Yazid did not exist then the patience, thanks, resolution and perseverance of Imam Hussain ﷺ would not have been known.

Like this all the deniers and rejecters of the prophets, Awliya Allah, the deniers of the blessed Companions and the Ahl al-Bayt and the four Imams of Fiqh were created for a reason. The deniers of these blessed and chosen people continue to deny while those who believe do so and recognise their glory and honour in the light of the Qur'an and Sunna. The greater the denial the greater the status and honour of these people is known. The darker the night sky the more the stars shine. Just as the black night sky is needed for stars to shine, so does goodness need evil to oppose it so that the Truth can be known for certain.

It was a few years ago when on the twelfth of Rabi al Awwal that the annual procession (*Julus*) to celebrate the Mawlid un Nabi took place in Kotli Loharan Sialkot. The procession was about to set off when it started to rain very heavily. It rained so much that it looked like it would never stop. The heavy downpour led to some of the people to call for the postponement of the procession due to the weather. But an incident took place that meant that the procession took place that year with more passion than ever before. The reason for the change of mind was the comments made by some deniers and rejecters of Mawlid un Nabi. They began to say that doing such processions is a bad innovation and that it was Allah's wish that the procession did not take place, hence the reason why it began to rain heavily. The people of Kotli Loharan, Sialkot are witness to the fact that these words uttered by the deniers of Mawlid Sharif had such an effect on us that we decided to go ahead with the *Julus* at all costs. The procession that year was such a memorable one that will be remembered by everyone present for years to come. The heavens were open but the Kotli Mawlid *Julus* took place as planned much to the dismay of those who thought it was an innovation. Peoples ankles were covered in water, the rain would not stop. *Durud* and *Salaam* was being read and proclamations of *Takbir* and *Risalat* were being made. Wherever one looked there was water but there was also beaming and happy faces celebrating the Mawlid of their dear Prophet. That day, if the deniers had not said anything then the Mawlid *Julus* might not have taken place. We learn from this that rejecters are not made in vain.

"O Lord! You have not made anything futile."

A wise person in a gathering once said: "May the Almighty keep the non-Muslims safe and secure as they are a blessing for us." The people present were amazed and shocked by what the man said and asked him to explain. He said that if it were not for them then there would be no one on the battlefield to fight against. So how does one become a *Ghazi* (warrior) if there is no one to fight? And if there is no fight, how could one become a *Shaheed* (Martyr)? To become a *Shaheed* and a *Ghazi* is a great status in Islam. But how does one attain this status? It is only through the presence of the non-Muslims. If there are no non-Muslims then how do we become fighters and martyrs? We learn from this that even non-Muslims are a blessing for us. May Allah keep them upright and firm!

From this introduction we learn that the Pharaoh was the enemy created for Musa and Nimrod was the rejecter of Ibrahim. Abu Jahl was the great enemy of the final Prophet. Shaytan is the enemy created who opposes Allah. When the Prophet left this mortal world, his enemy Abu Jahl perished before him. When Ibrahim﷽ passed away the animosity of Nimrod had ended before that. When Musa left this world the Pharaoh had perished. When Imam Hussain was martyred, Yazid was also finished. They all have come and gone, but Allah Almighty remains and will remain so and so is His enemy Shaytan. Allah is eternal and without end. He has no begin or end. He has also created an enemy for Himself. The animosity facing Him is by far the greatest and longest as Allah has appointed a certain time for him. *"You are given a time."* (7:15)

Allah has delayed his punishment and has also given him some powers so that he can try as hard as he can to derail people off the right path. The people who believe in Allah and avoid Shaytan's devious schemes will be rewarded with eternal bliss in paradise. The people who do not believe in Allah and fall into the Devil's trap will suffer eternal punishment in Hell.

The party of Allah (*Hizb Allah*) and the party of the Devil (*Hizb al-Shaytan*)

Allah has sent messengers and Holy Books with guidance for mankind so that they can know their Lord. For those who reply to the call of Allah there is paradise in which they will live in forever. Shaytan too has prepared ways for calling people to his final abode. Shaytan has spread his ideas of the worldly pleasures and comfort in this mortal world. Who are Shaytan's representatives and what are his ideas? Read the stories presented in the following pages and see how this cursed being has prepared programmes to deviate mankind from worshipping Allah and how he intends to increase the membership of his Party (*Hizb*). One of the wisdom's of Shaytan's creation is that he tries with all his powers to lure people to bad and evil ways so that the fortunate people can crush his movement and temptations and bring them back towards Allah. By doing this they earn a great reward from Allah Almighty. To avoid a temptation is only a good deed if the opportunity to do it arose in the first place. You would not marvel at a blind man going to the cinema and not seeing a movie because he does not have that ability in the first place. You would however marvel at a young Muslim surrounded by temptations all around him twenty-four hours a day and shuns them for the pleasure of Allah. Allah has created these plays and amusements for Shaytan so that Muslims can learn to avoid them and reject them and turn themselves towards Allah and in the process earn a great reward.

Sultanul Wa'izeen Maulana Abul Noor Muhammad Bashir

Shaytan's defiance

Allah Almighty ordered all the angels to prostrate to Adam ﷺ **all of them did except Iblis (Shaytan). He refused to do so and remained defiant. All the angels were in prostration but Iblis had his back to Adam** ﷺ**. When the angels lifted their heads from prostration they saw his defiance. Realising the situation, all the angels prostrated again in thanks that they managed to obey Allah.**

(Qur'an, 7 : 11, Tafsir Ruh al-Bayan)

Shaytan's pride prevented him from prostrating to Adam ﷺ. He thought that he was better than him and it was on this basis that he rejected Allah's orders and remained defiant. The angels obeyed Allah's orders immediately and without hesitation but Iblis did not. In Salah we prostrate twice in imitation of the act of the angels.

Shaytan's Philosophy

Allah ordered all the angels to prostrate to Adam ﷺ and all of them did except Iblis (Shaytan). Allah asked Iblis why he did not do as he was told. He said "I am better than him because you have made me out of fire while you have created him out of clay. Fire is light and bright, while clay is thick, dirty and depressing. So why should I bow down to something dull and opaque while I am exquisite and bright?" Allah did not like what Iblis said and expelled him and cursed him forever.

(Qur'an, 7 : 12, Tafsir Ruh al-Bayan)

Shaytan presented a philosophy explaining why he rejected Allah's command. His philosophy was the cause of his expulsion from the heavens. A closer look at his philosophy shows that his ideas were flawed. His thinking was wrong because it is Allah who decides what is excellent and superior. Excellency and superiority is gained through obedience not through what one thinks they are. Shaytan is wrong to think that fire is better than dust. From fire we have fierceness, rage and restlessness. And it is from these things that create pride and vanity. This is the reason why pride and vanity developed inside Shaytan preventing him from prostrating to Adam ﷺ. From clay however we get calmness, relief, patience, humility and modesty. Allah loves these attributes and it was these virtues that allowed Adam to seek Allah's forgiveness. Clay is superior because in paradise the soil there will be better than musk. There will be soil in paradise but no fire. Furthermore fire is a form of punishment and dust is not. The ground is the place for prostration, fire is not. The land is made of soil and clay. Fire is a thing that comes and destroys it and causes harm like forest fires. Valuables and goods can be kept in the ground or in things made of soil and clay but fire consumes and destroys everything that comes in its path. But the real crux of the matter is that dust &

soil can put out fire but fire cannot put out soil or dust. We learn from this that Shaytan's philosophy is totally false. The biggest mistake Shaytan did was to present this philosophy to Allah and to stick by it that caused him to be cursed and rejected until the time Allah has appointed for him. We should take note of Shaytan's philosophy, learn from it and avoid it at all costs. We should obey Allah's commands as the angels did and not to present false philosophies and excuses as the cursed Iblis did.

• 3 •

Shaytan's Vow

Allah expelled Shaytan from the heavens and cursed him. Shaytan asked Allah to give him respite and a deferment of punishment till the Day of Judgement. Allah granted his wish. Shaytan then vowed that he would sit waiting on the straight path and would

surround the children of Adam and take them off the path of salvation. He vowed to attack them from the front, from behind, from the left and from the right and make them his friends and ultimately ungrateful to the Almighty. Allah expelled him and declared that whoever followed the path of Shaytan would also go to Hell.

(Qur'an, 7 : 13-18)

Shaytan has made it his vow that he will take with him to Hell deniers and rejecters of Allah's supreme commands. He will do this by surrounding the people from all four directions. Those who follow this path are ruined. His mission is to humiliate the children of Adam. Fortunate are those who avoid his evil, wicked and tempting ways, and woe to those who fall into his nasty trap. Muslims in order to avoid his vow should be ready, prepared and alert at all times so that they can avoid Allah's wrath.

Shaytan's Whisper

Allah Almighty told Adam ﷺ and his wife Hawwa (Eve) to stay in paradise. They were allowed to go wherever they wanted and eat and drink whatever they wished. But He also ordered them not to go near a particular tree. Adam and Eve enjoyed the pleasures of paradise. Shaytan however came and put ideas into their minds about the tree that they were told to avoid. Shaytan told Adam that if they ate from that tree then like the angels they would no longer have to eat and drink. Shaytan swore on Allah's name and told them that eating from the tree would be good for them. Adam heard Shaytan swear on Allah's name, which convinced him that he was speaking the truth. Adam had no suspicions of what Shaytan had said because he felt that if someone swore on Allah's name, he must be telling the truth. This is why he accepted Shaytan's word. They ate from the forbidden tree. When Adam and Eve ate from the tree the clothes they wore disappeared and their nakedness became apparent to each other. To cover their private parts they used fig leaves. Allah told Adam and Eve not to eat from the tree. "Did I not tell you that he is your enemy?" Adam and Eve regretted their actions and realised that they had wronged themselves. Many years later Adam ﷺ on earth raised his hands in supplication and said:

"O Allah! I seek from you for the sake of Muhammad ﷺ that you forgive our mistake"

Allah heard this plea and forgave them both for their slip.

(Qur'an, 7 : 19-23, Khaza'in al-Irfan)

Shaytan made up false oaths to get revenge on his enemy Adam. Shaytan wanted Adam and Eve to be humiliated and ashamed just as he was. Adam ﷺ trusted what Iblis had to say because he said Allah's name. We learn from this that it is Shaytan's habit that he uses the name of Allah by swearing false oaths to lead people astray. Hence all Muslims should be aware of people today who hold the Qur'an in their hand and swear on Allah's name, as they are not necessarily truthful and sincere! We also learn that where Shaytan swore that there would be good there was in actual fact bad. Shaytan vowed that he would lead astray those on the straight path. We also learn that Shaytan's wishes us to do such acts that expose and humiliate us. He wishes to expose our nakedness at all times, he likes nudity. Hence we can see that in today's world the work of Shaytan is being done in a number of shameless and disgusting ways. When Adam and Eve covered themselves in figleaves to cover their shame, we learn that it is human nature to hate nudity and to dress modestly. Furthermore the forgiveness of Adam's mistake was due to him taking the intermediary of Prophet Muhammad's name. It is human nature-the way of Adam- to seek an intermediary. Such acts are liked and accepted by Allah, who is all Forgiving all Merciful.

Shaytan's Requests

Shaytan on the brink of being expelled from the heavens made a series of requests to Allah. He said "O Allah! You have rejected and cursed me, but at least grant me full power over the children of Adam so that I can lead them astray." Allah gave him such power. Shaytan asked for more and was granted a share of their wealth. Shaytan asked for more and was granted permission to live in the hearts of the children of Adam.

Adam ﷺ petitioned Allah and said "O Lord! You have granted the Devil so much power and domination over my children. How can my children possibly survive after his deceit and dishonesty? Allah told Adam that every child of his would be born with such a powerful angel that will protect it from Shaytan's endeavours. Adam asked for more from Allah and was informed that every good deed done by his children would be rewarded with ten good deeds. Adam ﷺ again asked for more when Allah told him that he would never take away from his children the ability to ask for forgiveness as long as they were alive. Adam asked for more when his Lord told him that the crown of forgiveness would be placed on mankind's head. Adam ﷺ was pleased with what his Lord had granted his children and did not ask for anymore.

(Nuzhat al-Majalis)

Shaytan's requests were accepted so that Allah's truthful men and women could endeavour to do good deeds and actions. If Shaytan did not have power over the children of Adam or a share in their wealth or stay in their hearts then there would only be good in this world without endeavour and hard work. For goodness to appear and thrive so must the Devil have the ability to try and derail us off the straight path. If we hear that a thief might come at night to steal our possessions, we make every effort to protect our property. We even appoint a person to look after the property. Like this, Allah has given Shaytan permission to roam around like a thief who will try and steal our faith away from us. It is by following the true teachings of Islam that we can keep safe and secure our faith from the Devil. We learn from this story that Allah has been very merciful upon mankind as they have the means of surviving the attacks of Shaytan. When we try to avoid the plots and schemes of Shaytan Allah becomes pleased with us. This is why He has promised the reward of ten deeds for doing one good deed. He has left the door of forgiveness open right until we draw our last breath. Allah according to His promise will forgive such a person but those who fail to grasp this opportunity in their lifetime are doomed in the hereafter.

Shaytan's Helpers

Shaytan on being expelled from the heavens made the following request to Allah.

Shaytan: O Allah! You will send Messengers and Prophets to guide mankind and you will reveal books upon them. What will be my books and who will be my Messengers and helpers?

Allah Almighty: Your Messengers will be soothsayers and your books will be false ideas, false words and poetry.

Shaytan: Who is my muezzin?

Allah Almighty: Singers will do your calling.

Shaytan: And what of my place of gathering?

Allah Almighty: Your place of congregating is the markets and bazaars full of dissension.

Shaytan: And what of my food?

Allah Almighty: The food on which My Name is not taken will be your food.

Shaytan: And my drink?

Allah Almighty: Intoxicants are your drinks.

Shaytan: And what will be my trap?

Allah Almighty: Your trap will be women.

(Nuzhat al-Majalis)

To make false claims and statements, to read false poetry, to sing songs and lyrics, to leave the mosque in favour of the shopping centres and markets, to have no care about Haram and Halal, to consume alcohol and to look at and entertain shameless women is Shaytan and his followers way of living. Shaytan is a liar and hence so are his evidences and ways of thinking. He and his followers make false assertions that confuse and harm people. For example in 1960 when I returned from Hajj I was in Karachi where there was a lot of commotion and worry amongst the people. I enquired about the fears of the people when I learnt that an Italian astrologer claimed that the world would end on July 14th 1960. A lot of people read and heard what this person had to say and became genuinely worried that the Day of Judgement was upon them. Businesses shut down as a result. I reassured people who I met that such talk was nonsense because in the Qur'an Allah Almighty says that the Day of Judgement would come suddenly and unexpectedly. If someone was told of the date of Judgement Day then it is no longer sudden and unexpected. This is just one example of false claims and assertions made by people that make the Devil happy. Muslims should have absolute faith and certainty about what Allah and His beloved Prophet ﷺ have told us and ignore immediately any false and unsubstantiated claims. False poetry should be avoided, as this is a trap of the Devil.

Songs and music is the Devil's call. Those people who respond to music and dance are hence the Devil's followers and reply to his evil call. The Devil's place of worship is the market and shopping centres. Allah's Azan happens in the mosque, and Shaytan's call takes place in the market and shopping centres. The food we eat and the fluids we drink must be Halal and secondly we should recite *Bismillah* whenever we start to consume food and drink. If we forget to say it at the beginning but remember during the meal then this is better for us. We must avoid alcohol, drugs and other intoxicating substances. Moreover we should keep our women dressed modestly and with respect. We should avoid seeing shameless women who are the trap by which people are put into humiliation.

• 7 •

Shaytan and Nuh's ﷺ Ark

When Sayyiduna Nuh ﷺ embarked on his Ark with his followers he saw a strange figure lurking inside his ship. He recognised him and realised that Shaytan was onboard. Nuh ﷺ asked him what he was doing?

Shaytan replied that he had come to put doubt amongst his people by entering their hearts and minds. Nuh ﷺ told Shaytan to leave the ship immediately. Shaytan said to Nuh ﷺ that there are five things by which I destroy the children of Adam. I will tell you three of them and not the other two. At that moment Nuh received a revelation from the Almighty in which he was commanded to ask for the two he was hiding and not the three he was disclosing. Nuh told Shaytan to tell him the two things he wished to hide, as he did not want to know about the other three. Shaytan then told Nuh ﷺ that one of the two things he uses to destroy men and women is jealously because that was the cause of him being rejected by Allah and the second thing that he uses to destroy mankind is greed. This is because man (i.e. Adam) was given the entire heavens but Shaytan managed to place greed into him that made him squander it.

(Talbis Iblis)

Jealously and greed are two powerful weapons used by

the Devil which he uses to destroy mankind. Jealously was the thing that made him hate Adam 🕊 and prevented him from prostrating. Jealously destroyed Iblis and he wishes to use that same weapon to destroy the children of Adam. Hence whenever Allah sent a Prophet or Messenger towards mankind, Shaytan would spread jealously amongst the people that would lead them to become disbelievers. These jealous people would then work against Muslims and tried to destroy them too. Shaytan has spread jealously in people's hearts that oppose the noble Companions and the Ahl al-Bayt (May Allah be pleased with them) and the weapon of jealousy is still used today. We see today people who oppose and challenge the respected elders of Islam and the qualified and pious scholars. To avoid the path of jealousy Allah revealed the verse *"And [I seek refuge] from the evil of the of the envious when he envies"* (113:5)

Greed is the second weapon of Shaytan. It destroys the rights of Allah and the rights of mankind. Greed results in people taking no care in respect to Halal and Haram.

Bribes, treachery, corruption and usury are all the direct results of having greed.

· 8 ·

Shaytan and Musa عَلَيْهِ السَّلَام

Sayyiduna Musa عَلَيْهِ السَّلَام met Shaytan who said to him "O Musa! Allah has chosen you as one of his messengers and has made you His Kaleem (the one who spoke directly to Allah). I am part of Allah's creation and I have committed a sin. I now wish to repent. Please could you plead to Allah on my behalf and get Him to forgive my mistake so that He can be happy with me again." Sayyiduna Musa عَلَيْهِ السَّلَام then spoke to Allah telling Him that Shaytan wished to be forgiven for his disobedience. Allah told his Messenger that His displeasure with him was due to his rejection of Adam. He did not prostrate to him when He commanded him to do so. If Shaytan wished to sincerely apologise for his sin then he should go to the grave of Adam ﷺ and prostrate to him. If he did that then Allah would forgive him. Musa ﷺ told Shaytan what Allah had to say. Shaytan replied, "Leave it. If I did not bow down to him when he was alive what makes you think that I will bow down to him when he is in his grave? This will never happen. I do not repent."

(Talbis Iblis)

Shaykh Safoori ﷺ quotes a narration from Nafsi that on the Day of Judgement Shaytan will be called from the Hell fire and Adam from paradise. Allah will say to Shaytan that if you prostrate to him now I will forgive you and you can enter the heavens but Shaytan will reject this ultimate offer saying that if he were to prostrate to him he would have done it in the first place *(Nuzhat al-Majalis)*. So we can see then that even despite being in the Hell fire, Shaytan will refuse a chance to enter paradise by refusing to bow down to Adam. Muslims should learn an important lesson and that is that we should respect and honour Allah's chosen and guided people and that we should never ever show defiance against them as Shaytan did otherwise our destiny will be that of the accursed.

9

Shaytan and
maintaining good actions

Once Musa عليه السلام asked Shaytan to tell him those things that he does that makes him overpower and dominate people. Shaytan told Musa عليه السلام that when a person thinks big of himself and thinks that his good deeds are a lot and count for something and he forgets his sins and errors, there are three things which they should fear at all times. The first is being alone with strange women. This is because when a man is with a strange woman, they are not alone because I am the third being with them. I put ideas and schemes into their hearts. The second thing is that when a person makes a promise to Allah they should honour it. This is because I accompany promises to Allah and act as barrier between it being fulfilled and the third thing is that when a person starts charity (sadaqa) they should maintain it because when they do not I stand in the way of it being fulfilled and carried out. Shaytan went away and then then realised what he had done and said "Oh no! I have told Musa my secret. Now he will go and warn the children of Adam about it."

(Talbis Iblis)

To think that you are someone special and important is what exactly what destroyed Shaytan. He thought himself to be beter than Adam 🕊. Islam teaches humility and modesty but worldly affairs teach egotism and arrogance. This is the reason why worldly-minded people look at people of religion with contempt and disdain. This contempt and disdain makes Shaytan happy. We should never think having done a good deed that we have done something great or extraordinary. This is because even if we spent every moment of our lives in Allah's remembrance it still adds up to very little. In every state we find ourselves, we should do good deeds but also rely on Allah's special favours and mercy so that no pride develops within us. Even if we pray five times a day this is very little, because the respected elders before us not only prayed the five compulsory prayers but did a lot more. If we think along these lines then the good deeds we do will not be regarded as a lot but very little indeed. To sit alone with strange women is inviting trouble from Shaytan. We should strive effortlessly to fulfil all our vows and promises to the Almighty. And finally we should not delay in giving charity in the way of Allah. Charitable donations and acts are to Shaytan what a saw is to a piece of wood. Hence we should strive to bring Shaytan down to size by using this invaluable saw against him.

10

The Devil's Friends and Foes

Allah ordered the accursed Devil to go in the presence
of His beloved Prophet ﷺ and answer any question
asked of him. Shaytan did as he was told and appeared
in front of the Prophet in the form of an old man. The
Prophet of Allah asked the old being who he was? The
person said that he was Iblis (Shaytan). The Prophet
then asked him why he had come. Shaytan told him
that the Almighty had sent him and was commanded
to answer as asked. The Prophet of Allah said, "Tell
me who your enemies from my Ummah are? Shaytan
said that he had fifteen enemies. The Prophet asked
whom they were to which the Devil gave the following
list:

- My first enemy is you
- A leader who does justice

- A humble man who has wealth
- A truthful trader
- A God-fearing scholar
- A good counsellor and friend
- A soft hearted believer
- A repentant
- A person who avoids Haram things
- A person who always stays in Wudu
- A person who does charity
- A person who keeps good morals and character
- A person who gives advantage to others
- A person who recites the Qur'an
- A person who gets up in the night to pray

The Prophet of Allah then asked him to reveal who his friends were? Shaytan said that he had ten types of friends. They are:

- An oppressive leader
- Arrogant and deceitful people
- Wealthy people

- **People who drink intoxicants**
- **Tale-tellers**
- **Vain people and show-offs**
- **People who take usury**
- **Those who take away the wealth of orphans**
- **Those who do not pay Zakah**
- **Those who have lots of desires**

(Tafsir Ruh al-Bayan)

On the request of the Prophet ﷺ, Shaytan revealed his friends and foes. We should all examine carefully this list and see where we fit into it. Are we in the list of his foes as we should be or are we in actual fact his friends and supporters? Ask yourselves which list should we be in? We all claim to be enemies of the Devil but only a deeper look at ourselves can answer this question. If I was to ask an audience whether or not they are with or against Shaytan everyone would unanimously say that they are against him. This is how it should be as Allah tells us that he is our open enemy. So we have established that he is our enemy and we are his enemy. So tell me are we Allah's friend or enemy? The response would again be unequivocal and that is that we are His friends and followers. So answer this question. The cinema and theatre is the home of the Devil, the enemy's home. The mosque is Allah's home, the friend's home. Everyone knows that if you are a friend of someone you do not go to the enemy's house and that a person goes happily and willingly to the friend's house. The enemy's house is treated with hostility. That is the theory but the practice is unfortunately the opposite. We go to the enemy's house and spend our money there and spend hours and hours but the friend's house is left empty and ignored and when one does go to the masjid people wish to leave as soon as possible! You have never entered the friend's house and you have never left the enemy's home. What sort of friendship is this and what sort of enmity is this? May Allah make us sincere friends of His and sincere enemies of His enemies - Ameen.

11

Shaytan's Ball

Shaykh Abu'l Qasim Junayd ﷺ saw one night a dream in which he saw Shaytan completely naked. "Have you no shame?" screamed the Shaykh. Shaytan replied "Are the people around you human?" The Shaykh replied, "Yes they are." Shaytan said "If they were humans then just as a boy plays with a ball, then I would not play with them like a ball. There are however some people whom I cannot play with". Shaykh Abu'l Qasim asked him who they were. Shaytan said, "There are some people in the Shonayzia mosque who I cannot control. They were so pious and obedient to Allah that all my tricks fail to lure them and make me depressed." He woke up from his dream and went to that mosque. There he saw three men with their heads lowered. When I screamed, one of them raised his head and said "O Junayd! Do not be taken in by the

words of Shaytan." He said this and then lowered his head again.

(Rawd al-Riyahin)

Nudity is the desired clothing of Shaytan. Those people who wear the clothes of Shaytan (i.e. nakedness) are the ball and play of Shaytan. He plays with it wherever and whenever he wishes. Sometimes it is in the cinema, sometimes in the clubs. The ball of Shaytan can be found all over the world thanks to the "West" who have spread this satanic ball by various means. People who act as real humans will not be seen in bad places but will be found in places of worship and rememberance. Such people are disclosed with knowledge from Allah and nothing is hidden from them.

12

Shaytan and the Pharaoh

One day Shaytan went to the Pharaoh and asked him whether he really thought he was God? Pharaoh said to him that he did. Shaytan asked for proof when the Pharaoh called all his magicians and told them to perform their best magic and tricks. The magicians began to perform in front of them. As they were doing this Shaytan blew on them and the magicians were engulfed in light, and then he blew again and they were once again visible. Shaytan asked the Pharaoh, "Tell me is your magic greater or is mine?" The Pharaoh conceded. Shaytan said "O Pharaoh! Despite me having greater power than you and your magicians, Allah has not accepted me. And you being weak and pathetic claim to be a partner or equal to Him!"

(Nuzhat al-Majalis)

The Pharaoh claimed to be God on the strength of his magicians but Shaytan ridiculed such a claim and humiliated him. The following verse of the Qur'an comes to mind: *'The example of Shaytan is when he said to man "disbelieve" and then when he disbelieved he said "I am free of you, I fear Allah the Lord of the worlds.' (Qur'an, 59 : 16)*

• 13 •

Shaytan and the Prevention of Good Deeds

One day the Holy Prophet ﷺ was leaving the mosque when he saw the accursed Shaytan standing outside. The Prophet asked him what he was doing. The accursed told him, "Allah has ordered me to go and answer any questions you had."

The Prophet of Allah asked Shaytan, "Why do you

prevent my Ummah from praying in congregation? Shaytan replied "Ya Muhammad! When your followers set out to pray in Jama'at I feel sick and have a bad fever and I stay sick like this until they have returned home from prayers."

The beloved of Allah then asked, "Why do you not allow my Ummah to read the Qur'an?" The accursed replied "Ya Muhammad! When they recite the Qur'an I begin to melt and dissolve." The Holy Prophet then asked, "Why do you prevent my beloved Ummah from Jihad?" Shaytan said "O Prophet of Allah! When they set off to engage in Jihad my feet are chained like a criminal, and I remain captive until they return". The Noble Prophet ﷺ then asked, "Why do you stop my people from offering charity and alms?" The accursed Shaytan said "O Muhammad! When one of your slaves intends to give *sadaqa* a saw is put to my head which cuts me just as wood is when it is put to the saw."

(Tafsir Ruh al-Bayan)

Doing good deeds causes real pain and anguish for our biggest enemy Shaytan. He does not do good himself nor does he allow others to do so. Offering prayers with congregation inflicts the Devil with fever. The Islamic scholars and preachers encourage us to come to the masjid and to pray Salah with congregation. So whoever criticises them for doing this are unwittingly siding with Shaytan. Recitation of the Qur'an makes the heart of the believer soft and gives him fear of Allah.

"Allah has sent the best book that from beginning to end is alike (in beauty and fairness) having two fold descriptions (promise of reward and threat of punishment) at which do shudder the skins of those who fear their Lord, then their skins and hearts soften inclining towards the rememberance of Allah." (Qur'an, 39 : 23)

When the Devil hears the Qur'an being recited he burns just as metal does under intense heat. We should therefore avoid becoming those people who do not recite the Qur'an, or don't meet people who recite the Qur'an.

Moreover we should have a love and affection for the Qur'an. Otherwise if we have that burning sensation and hate within then Shaytan has overpowered us.

To go out in the way of Allah in battle (Jihad) also hurts the accursed very much. The warriors and fighters of the truth have the Devil under their control when they go out to fight in the way of Allah. This is why in recent times the term Jihad has come under scrutiny as the Devil fears the power and strength of the Muslims. Jihad is a struggle against ones self (*nafs*) as well as fighting the enemies of Islam on the battlefield.

• 14 •

Shaytan's Most Beloved Friend

Once the Prophet of Allah ﷺ saw the Devil and asked him, "Who is your close confidant?" Shaytan replied,

"The drunk and intoxicant." The Prophet of Allah asked, "Who is your guest?" the Devil replied, "The thief is my guest." The Prophet then asked, "Who is your messenger?" The accursed replied, "The magician and trickster." He ﷺ then asked, "Who is your friend?" He replied, "The one who doesn't offer the Salah." The Prophet of Allah then asked him, "Who is your closest friend?" Shaytan said, "The one who says bad of (Sayyiduna) Abu Bakr ﷺ and (Sayyiduna) Umar ﷺ."

(Nuzhat al-Majalis)

The friends of the Devil are clear to see from this narration. Most importantly we learn that those people who hold enmity against Sayyiduna Abu Bakr and Umar ﷺ are the Devil's best and closest friends. We learn then that love for them saves you from the Devil, and hatred and enmity will lead you to him.

15

Shaytan and Sayyiduna Yahya ﷷ

One day, Sayyiduna Yahya (Prophet John) ﷷ saw the accursed Shaytan. He saw him with many things hanging off him. Yayha ﷷ asked him "what are these things dangling off you?" Iblis replied, "These are the desires and lusts of the world with which I trap the children of Adam" Yahya ﷷ asked, "Is there anything hanging off you that you use against me?" Shaytan replied, "Yes, there is. Whenever you eat and your stomach becomes full, that is when I come and distract you from your prayer". Yayha ﷷ asked, "Is there anything else?" The Devil said no. Yahya ﷷ then told Shaytan "Never again will I eat with a full stomach."

(Talbis Iblis)

Materialism and consumerism has made the task of

Shaytan all the more easier and makes pleasing Allah Almighty even harder. In recent times, the Devil has found new ways of distracting people and making them forget Allah. All around the world there is a proliferation of hotels, restaurants, coffee shops and other places, which never existed before. Wherever you go, you see menus and posters for 'tea time', 'lunch time' and 'dinner time', where people are encouraged to eat abundantly. However, nowhere but inside the mosque will you hear the call 'prayer time'. Shaytan has distracted the vast majority of people by encouraging them to eat unnecessarily. This waste of time will never come back as the time to worship of Allah goes away. Allah Almighty has created us for His worship and remembrance, not to eat and drink all day, so that we become tired, lazy and forgetful of the Being that has given us the food in the first place. We need to understand that to eat and drink is so that we can live. But the purpose of life is to worship Allah.

16

Shaytan the Thief

Abu Hurayra ⬥ reported that 'Allah's Messenger ⬥ appointed me to guard the *Sadaqa (al-Fitr)* of Ramadan. Someone came to me and started taking handfuls of food of the *Sadaqa*. I took hold of him and said, 'By Allah! I will take you to Allah's Messenger ⬥.' He said, I am needy and I have many dependents, and I am in great need.' (On hearing his tale) I released him. In the morning, the Prophet ⬥ asked me, O Abu Hurayra! What did your prisoner do last night?' I said, 'O Allah's Messenger! The person complained of being needy and of having many dependents, so I took pity on him and let him go.' The Holy Prophet ⬥ said, 'Indeed he has lied and he will come back again.' So I was sure that he would come again due to the words of Allah's Messenger ⬥. The next night, I waited for him watchfully. The thief did come again and started gathering food. I caught him again and said that I would definitely take him to Allah's Messenger ﷺ. He begged, 'Leave me, for I will not come back again.' I took pity on him once more and let him go.

In the morning, Allah's Messenger ﷺ asked me, O Abu Hurayra! What did your prisoner do?' I replied, 'O Allah's Messenger! He complained of being needy and of having many dependents, so I took pity on him and set him free.' The Holy Prophet ﷺ said, 'Indeed he has lied and he will come back again.' I waited for him attentively for the third time (the next night). He did come again and started gathering food. I caught hold of him and said, 'I will surely take you to Allah's Messenger ﷺ and this is the last of the three times you promise not to return, yet you break your promise and come back.' He said, 'Please let me go, and I will in return teach you some words with which Allah will benefit you.' I asked, 'What are those?' He replied, 'Whenever you go to bed, recite Ayat al-Kursi till you finish the verse. (If you do so) Allah will appoint a guard for you who will stay with you and no Shaytan will come near you till the morning.' So I let him go. In the morning, Allah's Messenger ﷺ asked, 'What did your prisoner do last night?' I replied, 'O Messenger of Allah! He claimed that he would teach me some words by which Allah would benefit me, so I let him go.' Allah's Messenger ﷺ asked, 'What are those words?' I replied, 'He said to me; whenever you go to bed, recite Ayat al-Kursi from beginning to end. He further said to me 'If you do so, Allah will appoint a guard for you who will stay with you, and no Shaytan will come near you till the morning.' Allah's Messenger ﷺ said, 'This time he told you the truth, although he is an absolute liar. Do you know with whom you were talking during these three nights, O Abu Hurayra?' 'No' I replied. The Messenger ﷺ replied, It was Shaytan.'

(Sahih al-Bukhari)

To steal is Shaytan's way. We learn that when the accursed is caught he makes up lame excuses and gets away from softhearted Muslims. Shaytan made the most of Abu Hurayra's humanity. What the accursed said about *Ayat al Kursi* was absolutely true but despite that he is still a great liar and deceiver. We learn from this that not every person who preaches speaks the truth. Because on some occasions the speaker maybe Shaytan himself. Hence Muslims need to be on their guard as to who preaches them about Qur'an and Hadith because, as the story indicates, they may tell you some good things but their main aim is to deceive and misguide you. Shaytan can take the form of humans too, so we need to be careful about whom we listen to. The story clearly indicates that the Prophet of Allah was fully aware of the intruder, who he was and that he would come back. So who says that the Prophet has no knowledge of the unseen?

Shaytan and Goodness?

It is written in *Kitab al-Arsh* that a person was sleeping underneath a crumbling wall, when the wall gave in and was about to fall on the sleeping man. All of a sudden, a person came and woke that person up and rescued him from the falling wall. The wall fell down and the man survived. The man shocked to see what happened looked gratefully to the stranger thanked him and asked him who he was? The stranger replied Shaytan. The man was shocked to hear that the stranger was the accursed and said "Shaytan and goodness?" Shaytan said, "I know what the final Prophet ﷺ has promised for that person who is killed under a wall without knowing it. That person dies as a *Shaheed* (martyr) and is entered into paradise. I did not wish for you to die as a *Shaheed*."

(Nuzhat al-Majalis)

Shaytan and goodness? Everything Shaytan does is for his purpose only. A person who has fallen out of the pale of Islam but still claims to be a Muslim, may from the outside look good and pious but is in actual fact very dangerous. Many people are trapped and misguided by such people who are the Devil's friends and partners. When these people read the Qur'an even that is dangerous, as they use good means to trap them. After a while, they then indoctrinate and ruin these innocent people. The poisoned honey may taste sweet at first, but the after-effects are deadly.

• 18 •

Shaytan the Divider

Ibn Mas'ud ﷺ says that once Shaytan once passed such a group of people who were busy in the *Zikr* of Allah. Shaytan wished to put fitna (dissension) among them, but could not. He left them to see another group of people. This group was not busy in Allah's *Zikr* but were talking about worldly matters instead. Shaytan deceived and seduced them with his evil ways. The result of this was that the group began to quarrel and fight amongst themselves. They quarrelled to the extent that they fought each other. The group busy in Allah's *Zikr* saw what was happening. They stood up and went to stop the fighting. But as they went to try and stop the bloodshed they got involved too.

(Talbis Iblis)

One of Shaytan's ways is to divide people by creating dissension amongst them. He makes Muslims fight amongst each other, which makes him very happy indeed. Shaytan has used this tactic in the past and uses it now and will use it in the future. Today, he uses the enemies of Islam to divide the Muslim world into small groups and countries. We learn from this story that those who are engaged in the *Zikr* of Allah are not deceived and hence divided by Shaytan. But as soon as they stop Allah's *Zikr* and come near those people who do not do *Zikr* then they too are engulfed and embroiled in Shaytan's web of deceit. So for Muslims to avoid Shaytan's tangled web of divide and rule, we need to busy ourselves in Allah's *Zikr* at all times. And moreover we need to avoid those people who have made the world their only affair. We also need to remember that to create dissension amongst ourselves is in fact doing the Devil's work for him. Shaytan detests to see the Muslims united. So we should strive to unite the true believers together at all times so that the Devil does not get an opportunity to weave his web.

• 19 •

Shaytan and Shaykh Abd al-Qadir Jilani

Shaykh Abdul Qadir Jilani ﷺ who is also affectionately

known as Al-Ghawth al-A'zam once saw a light that shone so brightly that the sky was engulfed in it. From the light a face appeared. The figure then spoke. It said "O Abdul Qadir! I am your Lord! I am very happy with you. Go! For I have made what was Haram for you Halal." Shaykh Abdul Qadir Jilani ﷺ heard the voice and read "I seek refuge from the accursed Shaytan." It only took these few words for that light to turn into darkness, and the figure turned into smoke. A voice then said "O Abdul Qadir! I am Shaytan. You have survived my trickery due to your knowledge and virtue. Otherwise you would have got caught in my scheme which would have led astray seventy devotees on Allah's path."

(Bahjat al-Asrar)

Shaytan is a crafty and shrewd imposter and a very deceitful being. To trap and mislead people he takes various guises and forms. He even pretends to come as the Almighty God. To escape from this trap of deceit knowledge and virtue is needed. Without it, stepping on the straight path, on which the Devil is sitting on and waiting, is very hard to cross and to remain firm upon. If some false Pir or Shaykh claims divine inspirations and contravenes the teachings of Shariah by not praying Salah, then assume then that such a person has fallen for Shaytan's plan which he tried to unleash on al-Ghawth al-A'zam ﷺ. We learn from this account that by simply reciting *Ta'awwuz* the accursed Devil is defeated and goes away. We must understand that Salah and other forms of worship cannot be performed only by the heart as some false Pirs and Shaykhs say. Salah is that which Prophet Muhammad ﷺ, his Noble Companions, his pure household and noble successors performed. Those people who say that keeping the beard is not necessary but only in the heart are also deceived. Islam is about the apparent and the concealed. Both have to be established and maintained to live according to Islam and to survive the onslaughts of Shaytan.

Shaytan's Depression

**Shaykh Hatim Asim ﷺ says that the accursed Shaytan
once came to him. He came with the hope of luring
me into the worldly ornaments of food, clothes and
shelter. But I gave him such responses that left him
defeated and depressed. People come and ask me what
he said and what I said in response. Shaytan said to
me "what will you eat?" I said "death!" (Allah says
in the Qur'an: every being will taste death). Shaytan
then said, "What will you wear?" I said to him "I will
wear the coffin shroud!" He then said, "Where will
you live?" I said to him "in the grave!" Shaytan heard
these three responses and become very depressed.**

(Tazkirat al-Awliya)

The accursed tries to lure us away from remembering
Allah by offering and tempting us with food, clothes and

shelter. There are many unfortunate people who have lost their faith and sold their faith in pursuit of these three things. But there are fortunate people who have not been lured by the Devils offer but instead have adopted the food, clothes and shelter which Islam alone provides. These people lived in weak houses but had strong faith. But the opposite is true today. We live in strong, solid and comfortable houses but our faith is very weak indeed. Similarly in previous ages houses were not well lit, but their hearts were illuminated. But today we see the houses are well lit and decorated but people's hearts are dark, void, and empty and with no hope at all. Despite worldly goods, people experience depression and lack of satisfaction. The remembrance of death brings you closer to Allah and safely away from the schemes of Shaytan.

Shaytan and the Rays of Ma'rifa

Abu Sa'id Khuraz ﷺ **says that once in his dream he saw Shaytan. He commented, 'I got hold of his stick and chased after him. Shaytan turned round and said to me "O Abu Sa'id! I am not scared of the stick you carry. If I am scared, then it is the *Arif billah* in whose heart is the sun. And when rays of light come from that sun of truth then I get very scared.'**

(Tafsir Ruh al-Bayan)

Ma'rifa (recognition) of Allah is such a great honour and strength that even the accursed Shaytan is scared of it and can do nothing about it. No power even military power can stop the forces of Shaytan. The West may have all the weapons they need, but they do not have knowledge and awareness of Allah. And until they possess this they will remain to be the slaves of the accursed and his way. The same applies to us Muslims who fail to try and recognise Allah Almighty.

• 22` •

Shaytan's Scream

When Allah Almighty sent the order for Salah to our beloved Prophet 🌺, Shaytan gave a very loud and painful scream. All of Shaytan's friends and accomplices heard his scream and came to his aid and asked him what the problem was. Shaytan informed them that Allah had prescribed Salah for the children of Adam. Shaytan said to them, "Wherever and whenever possible you must stop them praying Salah by keeping them busy in other things." The Devils asked their leader what would happen if they could not do that. Shaytan responded, "When they stand up for prayer then four of you surround them from each side: from the right, from the left, from above and from below. And when you do that call them towards you and distract them so that there is no sincerity and consistency in their Salah. Put ideas into their heads that they must complete the prayer quickly as they have other things to do. And remember! If despite that they remain steadfast and complete the prayer successfully then we are ruined. Because Allah will forgive such a person who prays their Salah."

(Nuzhat al-Majalis)

When the order for Salah came, Shaytan gave a scream. And whenever Salah is mentioned he screams and feels depressed. He thinks badly of those who call people towards Salah and pray it. Azan is the means by which Salah is publicised; therefore Shaytan does not like Azan. We learn from the Hadith Sharif that the Devil runs away when the Azan is called. Shaytan was a rejecter of Sajda (to Adam) and hence he is against Salah, because the centre point of Salah is the Sajda. He does not wish that we do Sajda in Salah because that would mean we do that act which he failed to do. We learn from this that as soon as the Azan is given, we should give up whatever we are doing and should run towards Salah and offer those Sajdas of thanks to the Almighty which the accursed Shaytan was not destined to do. Even when we stand for prayer, the Devil tries to put whispers and doubts in our minds. From the right and left he tries to distract us. But the Muslims are fortunate in that they pray with the presence of heart and mind intact and defeat the accursed Shaytan. The result of such a Salah is forgiveness from the Almighty.

• 23 •

Rahman and Shaytan

Allah ejected Shaytan from the heavens for disobeying his orders. Shaytan in response said:

...I will surely lie in ambush for them on your straight
path (to mislead them)
Then I shall certainly come upon them from before
them and from behind them, and from their right and
from their left...

(Quran, 7 : 16-17)

Shaytan had announced his plans to surround the
children of Adam from four directions. The angels
were worried by these developments and said, "O
Allah! Shaytan the accursed plans to destroy the
children from four sides" Allah told the angels that
two directions remained. "He has four sides but I have
protected two. When a child of Adam comes to Me
and prostrates and when they raise their hands in
supplication to Me, then I will grant their wishes and
will forgive their sins.

(Nuzhat al-Majalis)

Shaytan surrounds us from four sides at all times and
tries to lead us off from the straight path. He is trying

his utmost to make us rebels of Allah. But Allah's mercy is such that he has given us a way to protect us from the schemes of the accursed. The Devil attacks us from the right, the left, from behind and from in front. But Allah has protected the other two directions. They are above and below. To benefit from these two paths of salvation Muslims must establish the Salah so that our heads and lowered, especially in Sajda. Similarly we need to make the Du'a to the Almighty to forgive us by raising our hands upwards. By establishing these two paths, the Devil is defeated and helpless. There are very unfortunate people who have never prayed before, and who do not raise their hands in Du'a. These people according to this account have been well and truly trapped in Shaytan's ambush.

The Sufi people have said a very interesting point here. They say that out of the six directions possible only two are safe and secure. They are above and below. It is very difficult to keep our sights upward at all times as it is unnatural and difficult. The answer therefore is to keep our gaze looking downwards with humility and sincerity. Allah says in the Qur'an: "Say to the believers to keep their sights downwards." (Qur'an, 24 : 30)

• 24 •

Shaytan and Allah's Response

Sayyiduna Muhammad ﷺ said that when Allah ejected Shaytan from the heavens, Shaytan said to Allah, "O Lord! I swear by your honour that as long as your men and women live, I will continue to ambush them and lead them astray". Allah responded to this insult and said, "I swear by My *Jalaal, Azmat* and My loftiness! That whenever My men and women call Me and ask for forgiveness, I will respond to them and forgive them."

(Mishkat al-Masabih)

Shaytan is our greatest enemy and has vowed to be

hostile against us until our last breath. Allah however has vowed out of His mercy that as long as we live, and we ask for His forgiveness He will continue to forgive us. So it is a very unfortunate being that does not plead with Allah to forgive them as long as they live, and unwittingly supports Shaytan.

Shaytan's Scare

Before the appearance of Sayyiduna Muhammad ﷺ to the earth, the Devils and Jinns made a place near the heavens where they would stay. There they would hear the conversations between the angels. They would listen to these conversations and then add lies and twists to them and mislead the people on the earth by it. But when Sayyiduna Muhammad ﷺ was sent to the world as the final Prophet and he declared his Nabuwwa publicly, this privilege for the Devils and Jinns was stopped. They told Shaytan that they no longer had the privileges of eavesdropping on the conversation of the angels in the heavens. Whenever they tried to do that, flames of fire would prevent them.

One day, all the Devils and Jinns got together and went to see their leader Shaytan. They told him what was happening in regards to receiving news from the heavens and the flames of fire. Shaytan heard this and said that some important event must have happened on the earth. Shaytan ordered them to go across the earth and find wherever possible some sign or event which can explain why they were prevented from hearing news from the heavens. The Devils and Jinns heard this command and went about scouring the earth for evidence. The Devils and Jinns would bring soil from various parts of the world and bring it to Shaytan to smell. He would smell it and then throw it away saying that nothing new has come in this land.

But when a Jinn brought soil from the land of Makkah and gave it to Shaytan to smell his reaction was very different. He smelt the soil and became scared and said to them that something terrible has happened there. He ordered that they go and find out what has happened there. Shaytan sent nine Jinns who were respected and honoured leaders to go to Makkah to find out what was happening.

When the Jinns descended to the earth, they saw behind some date trees a man whose face shone like the full moon lead some other men in prayer. They were reciting something that they had never heard before. They came closer and heard what was being read. Sayyiduna Muhammad ﷺ was leading his beloved Companions in Fajr Salah. As the Prophet of Man and Jinn recited the Qur'an, the Jinns listened in silence and respect to what was being read. The recitation, which was being done by the best of creations ﷺ, had a great effect on the nine Jinns. Rather than gathering news on the events in Makkah, they became Muslims themselves as they submitted to Allah and His Messenger ﷺ.

This event is mentioned in the glorious Qur'an;

Say: It has been revealed to me that a party of the Jinn listened, and they said: Surely we have heard a wonderful Qur'an

(72:1)

The Prophet of Allah ﷺ taught them Islam and made them his religion's propagators.

(Sahih Muslim, Sunan al-Nasa'i, Mughni al-Wa'izin)

The Prophethood of Sayyiduna Muhammad ﷺ ended the privileges which the Devils and Jinns enjoyed previously. The declaration of his Prophethood made Shaytan scared. We learn from this that the Prophet's appearance (i.e. the Mawlid) makes the Shaytan and his associates uneasy. On the other hand, the people of faith and love become happy and ecstatic. We also learn that due to the presence of our Prophet ﷺ in Makkah that the soil became fragrant, which even the Devil could smell and recognise. The story also illustrates the power of the words of the Qur'an that had such a great effect on the nine Jinns. So whoever is not taken in by the recitation of the Qur'an is neither man or jinn but is instead worse than an animal. We learn that to have an effective recitation needs an effective mouth as well. If we recite Qur'an, but are not touched and affected by it, it is not the Qur'an's fault but ours. For example, a cartridge or bullet is only effective (and lethal) only if it is placed inside a gun and shot. If the bullet were thrown at someone then nothing would happen. But if the cartridge were placed inside the gun and shot then the bullet would have its desired effect. To make ourselves effective we need to adopt clean lifestyles and traits and these include eating Halal and Tayyib food and drink and to speak the truth. Adopting these ways will make our tongues more effective and penetrating. When we recite the words of Allah in this way, then we too would have the same effect on ourselves and on others as the Prophet of Allah had on the party of Jinns.

Samhaj the Jinn

Hazrat Amir ibn Rabee 🕮 says that once we were with the Prophet of Allah 🕮 in Makkah when a voice from the mountains said "People! Attack Muhammad." The Prophet of Allah 🕮 then said to us "This is one of the armies of Shaytan and whenever the accursed attempt to attack a prophet or messenger of Allah they are certainly killed." After a short while the Prophet of Allah said to us that a Jinn named Samhaj, but whose named he had now changed to Abdullah, killed that Devil." Hence we heard from the mountains a voice say, "We have killed Mushar."

(Hujjat Allah ala al-Alamin)

The enemies of the Prophet are always defeated and humiliated. The Devil has great disrespect and hatred for the Prophet and cannot bear to even hear his name.

But the slaves and lovers of the Prophet of Allah defeat these rejected beings. The beings that give support to the Prophet of Allah are not only humans but also Jinns. This is because he came to the world as the Prophet of man and Jinn ﷺ.

Shaytan and Sayyiduna Ayyub ﷺ

Shaytan once saw Prophet Ayyub ﷺ in devout and sincere worship to Allah Almighty which made him burn with jealously and anger. He tried his best to distract Allah's Prophet but failed to do so. Shaytan once said to Allah, "O God! Ayyub ﷺ who worships you a lot only does so because you have blessed him with wealth and children and so forth. His health is good that is why he always remembers You. If difficulties were to descend upon him he would never worship You in the way he does so now." Allah Almighty replied "Rejected being! This thinking of yours is entirely wrong. Go and I give you authority over his wealth, children and so forth and do as you please, and see how My servant does not change in his worship to Me."

Hence Shaytan went away with this authority and began to test Ayyub ﷺ. On the first day, he destroyed his offspring. On that day, seeing what had happened to his children, the Prophet of Allah displayed patience and thanks to the Almighty, and became busier in His worship. The next day, Shaytan destroyed all of his wealth by setting it on fire. And like before Sayyiduna Ayyub ﷺ displayed patience and thanks and began to increase his worship of his Lord. Ayyub ﷺ knew that whatever he had was from Allah and that if He wished He could take it away at anytime. On the third day, an illness struck Ayyub's ﷺ body that inflicted him with severe wounds. But despite such an unusual illness, there was no difference in his devotion to his Lord. Shaytan seeing that no difference had been made over

the last few days, went away depressed and defeated and had to accept that Allah's prophets cannot be undone by his tricks and deceits. Allah blessed Ayyub 🕊 **with a quick recovery from the illness and rewarded him with even more wealth, health and offspring.**

(Rawd al-Fa'iq)

Shaytan wishes that the people of Allah are involved and embroiled in problems and difficulties. And as a result of this they complain to their Lord and become heedless in His remembrance. The chosen men of Allah take on these challenges with patience and gratitude, and remain steadfast in whatever He gives them. Moreover these people never complain to Him nor do they slacken in His remembrance. This is in comparison to those people who when face a difficulty say "O Allah! Is there not a person in this city who deserved this more than me." People say statements of this nature that makes Shaytan happy, as people become ungrateful to Allah. The chosen people of

Allah take on these challenges with patience and thanks to Him and remain steadfast to whatever He gives them. The example of Ayyub ؏ given here is an exemplary one. And when we look at the history of this Ummah we see in the martyrdoms of Sayyiduna Uthman ؆ and Imam Hussain ؆ the same level of patience and thanks to the Almighty.

• 28 •

Shaytan and the Prophet's ﷺ Companions

When the final Prophet of Allah ﷺ came to this world, Shaytan sent a party of Devils to his Companions. Shaytan and his helpers would go to the Noble Companions but would come back defeated and disappointed. Shaytan asked them why they always

came back defeated and disappointed? They told him that they had never seen a group of people like them before. Shaytan consoled them by telling them that soon, they will gain conquests after which they would be able to influence them and distract them.

(Talbis Iblis)

Shaytan became defeated and disappointed by the Noble Companions. They are those people who spent their time in the holy and blessed presence of Prophet Muhammad ﷺ. Hence Shaytan cannot gain any influence over them. Shaytan hoped that he could influence them when they began conquering land. But even then Shaytan and his party could not get what they wanted. Shaytan attempts at all times to mislead the people of Allah but Allah protects them at all times.

29

Shaytan and Amir Mu'awiya

Sayyiduna Amir Mu'awiya ﷺ was resting at Fajr time when he heard a voice that said, "Get up! Offer the prayer with *Jama'at* otherwise your prayer will be missed." Amir Mu'awiya got up and looked in all four directions to see where this voice came from. But he could not see the being that told him to wake up. He then said aloud "O person who wakes me up! Who are you?" The hidden being said that he was Shaytan! Amir Mu'awiya was shocked to hear this and was bemused by what the accursed was inviting him to do. "O Shaytan! Your job is to keep people asleep and away from Prayer, why are you waking me up?" Shaytan then told him why he wanted to wake him up. "The truth of the matter is that last week when you missed your Fajr Prayer you began to cry. You cried so much that I heard from the angels of Mercy that Allah

liked your crying so much that He rewarded you with the sawab of seventy *Jama'ats*. I thought to myself that if you stay asleep today then you would start to cry and be remorseful like before and Allah will again reward you with seventy Prayers. So by waking you up you only get the reward of one *Jama'at* not seventy.

(Mathnawi Sharif)

Shaytan is a very clever, tricky and sly being. On some occasions he invites and lures people to do good so he can achieve his aims. He may invite towards good but the end result is bad. It is like honey mixed with poison. To invite someone to pray by *Jama'at* is a very good act indeed. But Shaytan's underlying aim was totally and utterly deceitful. We learn from this that sometimes, the Shaytan will admonish people about their obligations like Salah, but the end results of such actions is very dangerous. We learn from this that not every preacher is a good and sincere person, because they may well have their own hidden agendas. The preacher could be the Shaytan.

30

Shaytan and a Worshipper

In the community of Bani Isra'il there was a great worshipper. In his lifetime there were three young brothers. It just so happened that all three brothers were called up to fight in a battle. They could not find any suitable and responsible person with whom they could entrust their sister with while they went to fight. The three brothers after thinking long and hard suggested that they leave their sister with the worshipper. They recognised the worshipper as the pious and obedient one from Bani Isra'il. Hence they took their sister to the worshipper and requested him to look after her while they went away. But the worshipper refused and sought refuge from their sister and requested not to be asked again. But the three brothers insisted and the worshipper finally agreed to take care of her on the condition that she was left in a house across the road from his room of worship. The brothers finalised the arrangements and left their sister. The sister stayed in the care of the worshipper for quite some time. The worshipper would bring food for her and leave it outside his prayer room and call her to eat, he would then go back to his prayer room.

After a few days, Shaytan put ideas in the worshipper's heart that you give the young lady her food at your doorstep, why don't you drop the food off at her doorstep instead? Shaytan put the thought in his head that by doing this he would get more reward. Hence the worshipper began to take the food to her doorstep and called her to eat her food. After a few more days, Shaytan put the idea in his head that he should go inside and at least talk to her and ask how she is. By doing this, her solitude would go away and it would also earn him more reward. Hence the worshipper began to talk to the young lady when he went to drop the food off to her every day. The worshipper slackened in his worship and would sometimes spend the whole day talking to her. He would spend the day with her and then go back to his prayer room at night. After a few days after this happened, Shaytan again came to the worshipper and began to put thoughts about the young lady's beauty inside his mind. Shaytan's desired results occurred, and the lady became pregnant from the worshipper.

Shaytan again came to the worshipper and said to him, "What would you do and say to her brothers if they came back today?" Shaytan told him that he was worried that he would turn out to be disgraced and humiliated. Shaytan put the idea in the worshipper's mind to bury the child in the ground. The worshipper did just that. After that Shaytan came again and put doubts in his mind that the girl might tell her brothers when they come back about the whole story. Hence Shaytan put the idea in his head that he should kill her and bury her as well. After doing that the worshipper went back to worshipping in his prayer room.

After a long time the three brothers returned from battle. They went to the worshipper to ask him about their darling sister. The worshipper informed them that while they were away she had died. He took them to the graveyard and showed them her grave. The three brothers offered Du'a at her grave. The night they returned from battle, all three brothers had the same dream. In the dream they saw Shaytan in the appearance of a traveller. The traveller began to ask them about their sister. They told him that their sister had died. But the traveller told them that this was not the case, and told them the whole story. He told them that after they had left for battle, the worshipper slept with their sister, which resulted in a baby. The worshipper then killed the child and buried it. Then worried that she might tell you about the baby, he killed her too and buried her with the baby. Both bodies are buried in a pit in a corner of the house in which you last saw her.

The three brothers woke that morning and began to

tell each other about the strange dream they saw. All three brothers went to the house and dug the corner of the house to see the body of their sister and her baby. The three of them then went to the worshipper and then asked him to take account of what had happened. The three grieving brothers then went to the king to seek justice from the adulterer and murderer. The decision of the court was to hang him. When the convicted man was about to be hanged, Shaytan again came to him and asked whether or not he recognised him? Shaytan told the man that it was he that enticed him to touch the lady. Shaytan then told the man that he could help him escape from the hanging. The worshipper asked how he could do that. Shaytan told him to deny Allah. The misfortunate being did just that and left the fold of Islam. Shaytan then walked away leaving the disgraced man to face the death penalty.

(Talbis Iblis)

Shaytan's biggest trap against men is women. He uses

women to trap and destroy the biggest and brightest of personalities. That is why the Messenger ﷺ has ordered that women remain covered and that both men and women keep their gazes low at all times. Moreover he ﷺ strongly called for strange women and men not to sit together alone. We must remain alert at all times about this ever-present danger of being alone in the presence of strange men or women.

• 31 •

Shaytan and the Tree

The 'Proof of Islam' (Hujjat al-Islam) Abu Hamid al-Ghazali ﷺ says in *Ihya Ulum al-Din* that there was an worshipper who spent many years worshipping Allah Almighty. The people around him told him of a group of people that worshipped a certain tree. The worshipper heard of this and in anger and disgust at this decided to go and cut the tree down. As he was going to do that Shaytan dressed in the form of a Shaykh stopped him and asked him where he was going? The worshipper told the stranger that he was going to cut the tree down. Shaytan said to him, "You are a poor man, why do you need to go and cut this tree down. Why don't you spend that time and effort in *Zikr*?" But the worshipper replied that cutting down this tree would be counted as his worship to Allah. Shaytan then said to him that he would not allow him to go any further to cut down the tree. Having said that they both started to fight. The worshipper managed to pin down Shaytan and sat on his chest. The shaykh began to plead to him to get off him by saying that he wanted to say something to him. The worshipper got off him and allowed him to speak. Shaytan said, "Allah has not made it obligatory upon you to cut this tree down. And nor do you worship this tree. So why get involved? Are you some prophet who has been sent revelation to cut this tree down?" The worshipper heard what the Devil had to say but insisted that he would cut the tree down.

The two then started to fight again and like before the worshipper overpowered his opponent. The Devil defeated again, thought of another plan to get the worshipper not to cut the tree down. Shaytan said to the worshipper that he has come up with something that will distinguish between them and which would be beneficial for him. The worshipper was interested in what he had to say and asked him to elaborate. Shaytan said to him, "You are a poor man. Don't you wish that you have some wealth which you could spend on yourself and on your close relatives?" The worshipper admitted that he did sometimes wish that he had wealth so that he could enjoy life. Shaytan said to him to forget about cutting the tree down. Every night I will leave two Dinars underneath your pillow. Furthermore Shaytan said to the man that if he did cut the tree down, then those people would come along and start worshipping another tree, so what's the point in that? He started to tell him how he would benefit from having money. Slowly but surely the worshipper began to agree with the words of the Shaykh. He was no prophet and was not told by anyone to cut the tree and he would not be punished if he did not cut the tree. Or at least that is what he thought was the case.

The following morning the worshipper woke up to see two Dinars underneath his pillow. He saw this and became very happy. The next day when he woke up, he saw another two Dinars under his pillow. But on the third day when he looked under his pillow, he did not find the two Dinars, which he was promised. Angry by what had happened, he went off to cut down the tree. Shaytan again came in the form of a Shaykh and tried to stop him. Shaytan asked him what his intentions were. The worshipper told him to cut the tree down. The shaykh again said to him that he would not allow him to cut it down. Like before, they got into a fight. Shaytan this time grounded the worshipper and sat on his chest in victory. Shaytan told him to change his mind about cutting down the tree, otherwise he would kill him. The worshipper, puzzled and hurt by the defeat, asked the shaykh how he managed to defeat him this time when last time he was defeated? Shaytan told him that when he grounded him the other day, he managed to do so because he was fighting sincerely for the sake of Allah alone. But today, when he came to cut down the tree he came not with the sake of Allah in his heart, but the anger of not getting the promised two Dinars. The change in sincerity (*Ikhlas*) led to his downfall.

(Ihya Ulum al-Din)

Shaytan is extremely hurt by *Ikhlas* (sincerity). When a Muslim has this, then Shaytan cannot defeat them. We learn from this that without sincerity we cannot survive the onslaughts of Shaytan the accursed. If we have *Ikhlas* then Shaytan struggles in his tasks. That is why he tries to dent our sincerity. He puts ideas in our hearts and minds, drawing us towards the *Dunya* and worldly things and makes us forget about the *Akhira* and *Deen*. He creates desires for worldly things that make us greedy. When a person becomes greedy in this way, they cannot have any *Ikhlas* and hence his good deeds, if they have any, come to nothing. Salah is one of the biggest and rewarding good deeds possible. Allah instructs to 'pray to your Lord and give sacrifice (for Him and Him alone)' (108:2).

But if the daily prayer is done to show off then this is the example of those that 'are heedless in prayer' (107:5) and those that 'make show of their deeds' (107:6).

Finally we learn from this story that the duty to enjoin good and to forbid evil is for every Muslim, male and female. Doing so annoys Shaytan and pleases Allah.

• 32 •

Shaytan and Two Brothers

In previous times there lived two brothers. The elder

brother was very religious and worshipped a lot. The younger brother however was heedless of religion. The elder brother, one day, made a wish in his heart that he could see Shaytan. His wish came true and he saw the Devil. The Devil said to the worshipper that he came to him as he wished and now had a wish for him. Shaytan said to him that he had feelings for him that he had spent the last forty years in worship and obedience to Allah Almighty. Shaytan told the elder brother that he knew that he would live for another forty years. Shaytan suggested to him that he should spend the next twenty years of his life in joy and pleasure and to make a life for himself. He then said to him to then spend the remainder of his life repenting and worshipping, thus causing no harm. The worshipper liked what the Devil said to him, believing that he had half of his life ahead of him, and decided to see the rest of his immediate life in pleasures and joys of the dunya.

The elder brother lived in the upstairs apartment

while his younger brother lived downstairs. The worshipper having met the Devil decided that the best way of living a life of fun, pleasure and useless activities was to spend time with his younger brother who spent most of his time in such a lifestyle. While the accursed Shaytan was destroying the life of the worshipper, a change of thinking occurred with the younger brother.

The younger brother began to think and contemplate about his brother, how he spent his time in devotion and obedience to Allah Almighty. He then began to reflect on his own life and on how he spent it in worldly pleasures and activities. The younger brother made an intention that he would do sincere repentance (*Tawba*) and join his elder brother in being a worshipper.

The elder brother was coming down the stairs to meet his younger brother to inform him of his intentions, just as the younger brother was coming to do the same. The elder brother was walking down the stairs when his foot slipped causing him to fall down the stairs. The result of the fall was that he landed on his brother who was coming up the stairs. Both brothers got killed.

Allah Almighty decided on the basis of the respective intentions to punish the elder brother for his intentions and to place him with the bad people, and rewarded the younger brother with the company of the pious as a result of his good intentions.

(Rawd al-Fa'iq)

One of Shaytan's tricks is to convince people that they have long lives ahead of them in which they can enjoy the pleasures of the Dunya. Heedless people get caught in this trap and end up living sinful lives with no time or opportunity to repent to the Almighty. We learn from the story that when a sinful person repents sincerely and intends to visit pious people, then Allah the Merciful forgives their previous sins, and turns their bad deeds into good ones. Hence we should repent sincerely and keep the company of good and pious people as often as possible. We should attend such functions where such pious people are found. If anyone prevents you from going to such gatherings, then you must assume that such a person is a supporter and helper of the accursed Shaytan.

• 33 •

Shaytan in the Form of a Woman

In the times of Sayyiduna Isa ibn Maryam عَلَيْهِ السَّلَام there lived a very pious and devout woman. She had put her bread dough into the oven and began to offer her prayers. In no time at all, the accursed Shaytan appeared in the form of a woman and went near to her and began to say to her that her bread had burnt in the oven. But the devout lady paid no attention to the Devil whatsoever and continued her worship to the Almighty. Shaytan then took the lady's young child and placed him inside the oven. But again the woman showed no interest in what was happening around her. After a short while, the devout lady's husband appeared and saw his child playing with hot coals. The man saw this and went to Sayyiduna Isa ibn Maryam عليه السلام and told him about everything he saw. The Prophet of Allah told him to call his wife over to him. The man did as he was told and when the woman appeared before Allah's Prophet, he asked her what deed was behind everything described by her husband. The pious and devout lady said, "I always tries to remain in the state of ablution (*wudu*) and when it breaks, I performs it again and immediately offers two Rak'ats of prayer. And when someone asks me to do something, which I think Allah would also like, I carry that out. And I cope with people's troubles and afflictions and I remain patient about it."

(Nuzhat al-Majalis)

To pray salah hurts the accursed Shaytan a lot. He wishes at all costs that we do not offer Sajda, just as he did not. He wishes to accurse us too. He wishes to add such people to his party to go to the hell fire. Shaytan tries to prevent us from praying by putting ideas of dangers and worries in our minds, so that we stop the prayer, and become distracted. In today's day and age he achieves this by putting forward this "modern" idea that salah wastes time, and that time is money. But the true Muslim knows that such "modern" ideas are false and baseless, and would never ever leave his or her prayer at any cost.

We learn that to stay as much as possible in the state of ablution is an act very much liked by Allah. By staying in *wudu*, even hot coals cool down. And by coping with people's troubles and afflictions, Allah helps such people in their time of need. Patience is one of the best virtues which Allah loves dearly.

Shaytan, the Fasting Person and the Sleeping Person

An old man was approaching a mosque when he saw Shaytan at the door. The man was shocked to see him standing there. The old man approached the Devil and asked him why he was standing at the door? Shaytan said, "Look inside." The man looked inside to see a man praying and a man sleeping near to the door of the mosque. Shaytan continued, "I wish to put whispers in the mind of the man praying Salah, but I cannot enter the mosque because of the sleeping man. This is because he is fasting. When he breathes out, that air becomes flames of fire that hurts and prevents me from going inside. That is why I am standing here."

(Rawd al-Fa'iq)

Fasting is a great shield against the accursed Shaytan and his deceptive tricks. If a fasting person sleeps even that stops Shaytan in his tracks. Hence Shaytan worries a lot when he sees a fasting person. Moreover when a person gets worried or scared when the blessed month of Ramadan arrives that we should safely assume that that person is also Shaytan. This is because the Devil is shackled and imprisoned in this Holy month. Shaytan hates Ramadan and fasting while a Muslim should love Ramadan and fasting.

• 35 •

Shaytan and an Scholar

One day after Asr prayers, Shaytan sat on his throne. All the other Devils came to him and began to tell him what they had done that day. One Devil came up and said that he made so many people drink alcohol, while another Devil came up and said that he made so many number of people commit adultery. The Devils were telling their accursed leader, when one of them spoke up and said that he prevented a student from learning. Shaytan got up from his throne and went to embrace that Devil and congratulated him. All the other Devils where baffled to see what was happening as the accursed was ecstatic to see what this particular Devil had done. Shaytan sensing this sense of outrage told the other Devils that all their work was only possible as a result of this Devil's action. If they had knowledge they would not commit sins. "Let me tell you of a place where I will show you what I mean. A place where an worshipper lives but who isn't learned, and a place where a scholar does reside.

So one morning before sunrise, Shaytan and his followers arrived at this place. The followers hid as Shaytan stood on the street in anticipation of the worshipper. The worshipper was making his way to the Mosque for Fajr having prayed *Tahajjud* prayer earlier. The worshipper and Shaytan greeted each other. Shaytan then said, "Excuse me, could I ask you a question?" The worshipper said "Yes, you can but be quick as I am missing my prayer." Shaytan took out from his pocket a bottle and said, "Can Allah Almighty, if He so wishes, place the entire heavens and the earth into this bottle?" The worshipper thought for a moment and said, "How can it be that the heavens and the earth, which are so big, fit into such a small space?"

That was all it took for Shaytan to be satisfied as the worshipper left for his prayers. Shaytan showed to his followers how this worshipper questioned the power of his Lord. So what use was the worshipper's worship which he did?

Near to the time of sunrise, the scholar was on the street in a hurry. Shaytan stopped him and asked him the same question as before as he showed him the bottle. The scholar stopped and said, "Only Shaytan could ask such a question. This bottle is too big to fit the heavens and earth into it. If Allah wishes He could place the entire creation into the eye of a needle. He then quoted from the Qur'an "Indeed Allah is powerful over everything". The scholar left as Shaytan returned to his followers. "Did you see what benefit there is in knowledge. That is what prevented that worshipper from learning. What that Devil did was indeed a great act as it prevented him from attaining knowledge.

(Malfuzat of Ala Hazrat)

Knowledge of Islam is very valuable and important. That is why Shaytan is scared of the *Ulama* because they have the knowledge of how to stop and defeat him. Without knowledge, worship no matter how much it is, is always in danger. This is why Sayyiduna Muhammadﷺ him said "for Shaytan, one scholar is harsher on him than one thousand worshipper's". Or in other words Shaytan is not scared of a thousand Muslims than he is with one scholar. We learn from this that to fear scholars and to have animosity towards them is the work of Shaytan and that without knowledge, your worship remains in danger. This is because Shaytan can quite easily take that worship away by doubting our *Iman*. That is why Shaytan keeps pirs who have no knowledge far away from the scholar's. And that he makes such Pirs say that Shari'ah and *Tariqa* are separate things. "What do Molvi's know about *Tariqa*?" the absent-minded Pir says. If you come across such Pirs who say such things and contravene the practices of Islam then safely assume that such people are trapped in Shaytan's web. These Pirs believe that they have reached a station- but they do not know whether it is the garden or the hell fire?

• 36 •

Shaytan's Du'a

Sayyiduna Israfil ﷺ once read on the Preserved Tablet (*al-Lawh al-Mahfuz*) written that there will be a being whose thousands and thousands of years of worship would be wiped out and thrown back on his face. He read this and became scared that that being might be him and began to cry. All the angels gathered around Sayyiduna Israfil ﷺ and asked him why he was crying? He told them what he read on the *al-Lawh al-Mahfuz*. As a result all the other angels also began to cry. Angels were worried that that being might be them. They eventually decided to go to Azazil. Azazil was the former name of Iblis. He was held in high regard by all the angels for his worship. The angels decided to go to him and to pray for them that they were not the accursed being mentioned in the *al Lawh al Mahfuz*.

They went to Azazil and told him everything they read and happened. Azazil with humility said "O Allah be not wrathful upon him." Azazil prayed that the wrath and anger that was destined on somebody did not come upon Israfil ﷺ. The accursed thought of himself to be above doing a Du'a for himself and only prayed for the others. Hence Israfil and the other angels were

saved, and what was written on the *al-Lawh al-Mahfuz* also remained true.

(Nuzhat al-Majalis)

When we offer Du'a to the Almighty we should always put our position first. We should always ask Allah to forgive our sins and to pardon our mistakes. We should seek Allah's *Fadl* for ourselves at all times. Whoever prays for others, and overlooks their own position is copying Shaytan. If we were to spend our entire lives in worship, we should always be seeking Allah's mercy and always bear in mind of Allah's independence and carefree attitude if He so wishes. We should never think big of ourselves, no matter what other people think of us. We should learn from the example of Sayyiduna Muhammad ﷺ who is the king of innocence. Whenever he made Du'a he would always pray for himself and sought Allah's mercy. We too should follow this valuable and very important Sunna.

What Shaytan
said to the Pharaoh

One day, Shaytan said to the Pharaoh, "I am older than you, and yet I have never claimed divinity (to be God) how have you managed to claim it?" The Pharaoh thought about what was said and said, "Yes you are right, I seek forgiveness for doing so". "No! No!" Shaytan said, "Don't do that. The people of Egypt think of you as God. If you say that you are no longer God, they will not allow you to rule over them". Hence the Pharaoh stuck by his claim of divinity.

(Nuzhat al-Majalis)

Shaytan is the king of tricksters and deceivers. He made the Pharaoh a fool for claiming divinity and made him a bigger fool for attempting to distance himself from this false claim. Shaytan never had the ability to ask for forgiveness and also prevented the Pharaoh to do the same in his lifetime.

Who is Worse than Shaytan and the Pharaoh?

Once, the Pharaoh asked Shaytan whether or not there was somebody worse than they were? Shaytan replied "That person who is worse than us is the Muslim who does not accept the excuse provided by his Muslim brother."

(Nuzhat al-Majalis)

If a Muslim brother or sister for some reason presents an excuse then that excuse should be accepted. If not then that person become worse than Shaytan and the Pharaoh.

Shaytan and Anger

Shaytan once appeared before a Hermit. The Hermit asked the accursed "In the children of Adam, what act helps you to lead them astray and helps you in your cause?" Shaytan responded, "Anger is that thing which makes it easy for me to lead mankind astray, as easy as a boy who plays with a ball."

(Talbis Iblis)

Anger is a very bad thing indeed. Anger assists and helps Shaytan with his cause. When a person becomes angry they become fiery as fire is. Shaytan is also from fire, which is why it becomes easier for Shaytan to control them.

Sayyiduna Muhammad ﷺ has said:

"Anger is from Shaytan. And Shaytan is from fire. And fire is extinguished by water. Hence if you become angry, you should do ablution (*wudu*)."

(Mishkat Sharif)

Another Hadith states that, "If you are angry and you are standing sit down. And if you are still angry then lie down."

This means that sitting or lying down, which brings a person closer to the earth, extinguishes the fire of anger. This is because the earth (i.e. soil and clay) can put out fires.

40

Shaytan and his Five Donkeys

Sayyiduna Isa ibn Maryam ﷺ once saw the accursed Shaytan pulling along five donkeys. Sayyiduna Isa ﷺ asked Shaytan what they were. Shaytan replied, "This is my merchandise. I wish to sell it." Sayyiduna Isa ﷺ then asked, "Tell me what they are then?" Shaytan told him the names. "They are aggression, pride, jealousy, treachery and fraud. Aggression I sell to kings. Pride I sell to the leaders of towns and cities. Jealousy I sell to Qaris. Treachery I sell to traders and merchants. And fraud and cheating I sell to women."

(Nuzhat al-Majalis)

The five vices mentioned in the story are the merchandise of the accursed Shaytan. Every Muslim should avoid them at all costs. Very fortunate is that king who does not buy aggression (injustice) from him but instead rules fairly and equitably. And what can be said of that leader who buys this merchandise wholeheartedly and blindly. It seems that today the West has brought the whole donkey off Shaytan. They bomb and destroy other countries without any justification whatsoever.

Town and city leaders are also fortunate who do not act with pride and boast, but instead administrate with humility and equality. And like the kings, if they buy from Shaytan this donkey, then they destroy their own lives as well as that of others. This is because Allah despises those who show pride, as only Allah and Allah alone is allowed to display pride. The likes of Nimrod and the Pharaoh displayed pride and haughtiness and were eventually destroyed by the Almighty.

The Qari who does not become jealous is very fortunate not to have traded with Shaytan. The same can be said of that trader and merchant who has not dealt with Shaytan's donkey called treachery. And finally very lucky are those women who does not cheat others. They avoid deceptive behaviour and instead live lives of *Zikr* and *Fikr* like Rabia Basariyya 🌷.

• 41 •

Shaytan's Five Children

Zayd ibn Mujahid reports that Shaytan has five children. Its father has given each child a specific role. The names of the five children are Thabir, Aawir, Maswut, Wa-sim and Zuknabur.

Thabir's duty is dealing with problems and difficulties. He creates problems and difficulties for people that make them frustrated and make them lose all hope.

Aawir's task is to make people commit adultery. He makes people perpetrate this crime and humiliates them.

Maswut is entrusted with the duty of spreading lies and falsehoods. He listens to what people say and them takes that news and mixes it with false news to cause friction and dissension.

Wa-sim's duty is to enter people's homes with them. He highlights people's deficiencies and makes them angry. Zaknabur's duty is to be in the market place and shopping centres. There he unfurls his flag of Fitna and creates problems amongst the people.

(Talbis Iblis)

Just as we need to avoid the accursed Shaytan, so too must we avoid his five children. It is the work of Shaytan's children to be impatient when problems arrive, to speak lies and to spread them. So is to fight with family members for no reason; to commit adultery and to spread dissension in the marketplace. The wise person is one who avoids these traits. But the person who commits these vices is foolish no matter how much they maybe educated or civilised, simply because they have become the prey of Shaytan's wishes. Common sense is derived only from stability and perseverance in the practice of deen. Practising Islam will mean that one will avoid the practices of Shaytan and that of his children.

• 42 •

Shaytan's Grandson

Sayyiduna Umar Faruq ☙ **reports that one day, we were with Muhammad** ﷺ **on a mountain when all of a sudden an old man with a stick appeared and greeted the Prophet. The Prophet of Allah** ﷺ **suspected that the man was a Jinn which he was. The Jinn whose name was Hama was son of Haym whose father was Laqis who was the son of Iblis. Prophet Muhammad** ﷺ **confirmed from him that there were two generations gap between Hama and Iblis. The Prophet of Allah** ﷺ **then went on to ask him what was his age? "O Prophet"**

he said, "I am slightly less old than the earth. I was a few years old when Qabil (Cain) killed Habil (Abel). I used to run between mountains and steal people's food. I also put bad ideas about others in people's mind and sowed discontent and distrust amongst people". The Prophet ﷺ told him that his actions were wrong. The Jinn said he came to seek forgiveness. 'O Prophet ﷺ! In the past I met Nuh عليه السلام and spent a year in his company. I sought his forgiveness. Similarly I have spent time in the company of Sayyiduna Hud عليه السلام, Yaqub عليه السلام and Yusuf عليه السلام. I learned the Torah and sent Salam to Isa عليه السلام. It was Isa عليه السلام who told me to come to you O Prophet ﷺ and to offer his Salaam. So I am here to convey that message to you and I also request that you teach me some of the words of Allah. The Prophet ﷺ taught him Surah Mursalat, Naba, Ikhlas and Was-Shams. The Prophet ﷺ then said to Hama that he should come to him if he ever needed him. Umar states further that the Prophet ﷺ had left this world, and was unsure as to whether Hama was still alive or not.

(Khulasat al-Tafsir)

Sayyiduna Muhammad ﷺ is *Sayyidis Saqalain* namely master not only of mankind but jinn too. From mankind and Jinns there are those who love him a lot. We learn from the story that if your destiny is good, then even if you are the great grandson of Shaytan you can still be guided and saved. Similarly if your destiny is bad then nothing can save you even if your father is a prophet. The son of Nuh was amongst those who drowned in the floods. This is a clear sign of Allah's power, carefree approach and independence. From the dead He can create the living and He can also create the living from the dead. Indeed Allah is powerful over everything.

• 43 •

Shaytan in a Person's Dream

A man while asleep urinated in his bed. His wife, seeing what he had done said to him, "You wretched man! What has happened to you that you urinate on the bed?" The ashamed man told his wife what had happened. "I see Shaytan in my dream. We go for a walk, when I desperately need to go to the toilet. He sits me down somewhere and says 'urinate', so I do." The wife began to say to herself that Shaytan is from the Jinns, and Jinns have many powers. She told her husband that if the accursed appeared in his dream tonight, he should tell him that they are very poor indeed, and that he should help them financially. The husband agreed and said he would ask the Devil to help them if he appeared in his dream.

That night, the man in his sleep had a dream, and like the night before the accursed Shaytan appeared. The man said to Shaytan, "Every night you make me worried and frustrated. Please listen to what I have to say. I am a very poor man. I have little for my wife or myself. Please give us some money?" Shaytan heard this and became happy. "Why didn't you tell me this from the beginning? Come with me." Hence the accursed took this man to a place where there was lots of money. Shaytan said to the man to take as much money as he could carry. The man spread out a cloak and began to pile it up with money. The man filled the cloak as much as he could with notes and prepared to pick the bundle of money up. The money was so heavy for the unfortunate man that he soiled himself. The man woke up to see toilet covering his bed and not a single note or coin in sight.

(Taybah Monthly September 1971)

The world we live in is one of dreams and imaginations. And the wealth of this world is its toilet in which we are heedlessly lost. Shaytan stirs in our hearts and minds thoughts of amassing money and material goods. And it is by this means that he has us under his control. The accursed becomes very happy indeed when we get caught and trapped in this vicious and yet futile act. But when we open our eyes, namely when we taste death, we learn and realise that the wealth of this world is like toilet. Hence we should avoid the schemes and plots of Shaytan by

keeping our eyes open, firmly focussed on the hereafter
rather than this imaginary *Dunya*.

• 44 •

Shaytan and the Sacrifice of Sayyiduna Isma'il

Sayyiduna Ibrahim ﷺ in a dream was ordered by
Allah Almighty to sacrifice his only son, Isma'il for
Allah's sake. He saw this dream three nights in a row.
Prophet Ibrahim ﷺ seeing this divine order began
making preparations to sacrifice his only and beloved
son for his Lord's happiness and command. On the
third morning since the first dream, Sayyiduna
Ibrahim ﷺ told the mother of his son to bathe him
and to put new and fresh clothes on him. Sayyida
Hājar did as her husband ordered and prepared her

son Isma'il. Sayyiduna Ibrahim and Isma'il set off on their brief but decisive journey. Shaytan saw them set off, and became very worried indeed. He changed his appearance and went to Hājar and asked her whether she knew exactly what her husband was about to do to her only son? She said no. Iblis told her that her husband was taking Isma'il 卿 to be sacrificed. Hājar asked the stranger why this was the case? It slipped out of Shaytan's mouth and he told her that Ibrahim 卿 had a divine order to sacrifice his only son. Hājar spoke out and said that if that is the case then who are you to stop it? We are content with the will of Allah. Hājar had sensed that the stranger was Shaytan and she ordered him to leave immediately.

Shaytan left there and went to Isma'il 卿. Shaytan began to ask him whether or not he knew what was about to happen? Isma'il said no. Shaytan told Isma'il that his father was taking him to be slaughtered. Like his mother, Isma'il 卿 asked the question as to why, and like before the words slipped out of his accursed mouth that Ibrahim عليه السلام was acting under divine instructions. Isma'il عليه السلام heard this and said that if this is the case then who is he or anybody else to stop the will of Allah? The depressed and defeated Shaytan was recognised by Isma'il as he told him to go away.

Shaytan then made his way to Ibrahim عليه السلام and spoke to him. "Why are you acting upon something that you have seen in a dream that you are about to slaughter your only son? It was me who gave you that order, not Allah, do not carry out the commandment". Ibrahim عليه السلام realised what the accursed was trying to do and told him to go as far away from him as possible. He told the accursed that he would carry out Allah's command at all costs. Shaytan left hearing these words depressed and defeated as he failed to make any impression on them.

(Nuzhat al-Majalis)

Just as Shaytan hates Salah, fasting, Hajj and Zakah, he also hates it when Muslims men and women give sacrifice

(*Qurbani*) in the way of Allah. He wishes that no child of Adam give a sacrifice just as he failed to sacrifice his ego when he was ordered to do *Sajda* to Adam ﷺ. Sayyiduna Ibrahim ﷺ ignored the words of Shaytan and went ahead with the divine commandment. He followed the will of Allah, to which Allah became pleased, and replaced the intended sacrifice with a lamb from the heavens. Isma'il ﷺ was saved and yet the order of sacrifice was fulfilled. The Sunna of Sayyiduna Ibrahim ﷺ has been made necessary on the final Ummah as the Prophet of Allah ﷺ has ordered us to do so in the festival of Eid al-Adha.

Every year, Muslims over the world carry out this Sunna of Sayyiduna Ibrahim ﷺ and Sayyiduna Muhammad ﷺ As a result of this, Shaytan becomes depressed and defeated as he sees the children of Adam give sacrifice. But the crafty and tricky Shaytan tries to prevent us from doing the *Qurbani* by stating in various guises that the slaughter of millions of animals is wasteful and so on. Such people under Shaytan's influence say that it would be better to spend that money instead in some national fund for some other good cause. These types of voices are in reality the voice of Shaytan and try to stop sincere and honest Muslims from carrying out the Sunna. But Alhamdulillah the majority of the Ummah carries out this command with great commitment and enthusiasm every year.

We learn from this account that the dreams of Allah's prophets and messengers are in actual fact a form of *Wahy* (revelation). They are truthful and they do not resemble our dreams.

Sayyiduna Muhammad ﷺ once stated:

"In a dream I saw that the keys to the treasures of the earth were given to me and was entrusted with them"

(Mishkat al-Masabih)

If we are to believe the dream of Sayyiduna Ibrahim ﷺ to be true, then we must believe this dream to also be true.

Just as Shaytan tried to say to Sayyiduna Ibrahim عليه السلام that his dream was not true, there are today so-called Muslims who say that the Prophet of Allah is not the owner and possessor of the treasures of the earth, because they deny his dreams as narrated in Ahadith like the one above. These so called Muslims who do not believe in the authority and honour and esteem of Sayyiduna Muhammad ﷺ are just like Shaytan and try to mask the reality. True Muslims then should ignore the words and path of the accursed Shaytan and his associates and should instead believe whole-heartedly that Sayyiduna Muhammad ﷺ is *Ahmad-e-Mukhtar* : that Allah by His leave has given him wide authority over many issues.

• 45 •

Shaytan's Defeat

One night, Shaytan and his associates, hiding in the

jungle and mountains, sat about to try and defeat the final Prophet by attacking them. Shaytan in his hand had a burning torch with which he wanted to burn the face of Muhammad ﷺ (God forbid). In no time at all, Sayyiduna Jibril عليه السلام came and told the Prophet to pray the following Du'a:

'I seek refuge with the complete words of Allah from the evil that He has created, from the evil that descends from the sky, from the evil of the night and days discord and from the evil of every *Tariq* except the *Tariq* of good, O Rahman!'

The Messenger of Allah read those words, and no sooner did he read them that the torch of Shaytan was extinguished and was defeated once again.

(Talbis Iblis)

Shaytan is the biggest enemy of Sayyiduna Muhammad ﷺ and he remains troubled and hurt by his blessed presence. The Du'a that came out of the blessed mouth of the Prophet of Allah was a fatal one for Shaytan. Today, Shaytan wishes to attack the followers and ardent lovers of Muhammad ﷺ. So the best way for us to be protected from the accursed is to pray this Du'a when we go to sleep so that we can be protected.

• 46 •

Shaytan as Shaykh of Najd

One night the Quraysh 'enemies of the Prophet' met in a secret location where they were scheming to assassinate him. Abu Jahl, Abu Lahab, Utbah, Shayba and all the other Makkan chieftains were present as they sought to get rid of Muhammad ﷺ.

The confidential and private meeting was in progress when the accursed Shaytan appeared as an old man and knocked on the door asking them to let him in.

Not expecting any other guests, the people inside asked the person at the door who he was? Shaytan replied "I am a Shaykh from Najd, and I have come to participate in your scheme."

(Ghiyath al-Lughat)

The accursed Shaytan appears in every meeting where the honour and sanctity of the Noble Prophet ﷺ is attacked and defiled. He never ever attends those meetings and gatherings of blessings and honour where the praises of the Prophet of Allah ﷺ are heard.

We learn from this fascinating account that Shaytan has preferred to be associated with the province of Najd. He did not say at the door that he was a Shaykh from Iraq or from Yemen, or any other province, but chose Najd deliberately. The reason for this is quite clear. Shaytan chose Najd because animosity and hatred for the Prophet comes from there. The enemies of the Prophet live and come from Najd. Shaytan wishes to make clear his association with this region. By calling himself Shaykh of Najd, Shaytan has made clear that he is an open enemy of the Prophet, not a friend. If this were not the case, then the accursed Shaytan would have never called himself a Shaykh from that province.

• 47 •

Shaytan and the Holy Qur'an

A person was eating in front of Sayyiduna Muhammad ﷺ. The person had begun to eat and forgot to pray *Bismillah*. The person continued to eat without realising. He reached the last portion of the dinner when he realised he forgot to pray it when he said, *"Bismillahe Awwalahu wa Akhirahu."* He only took those words for the Prophet of Allah to laugh. He ﷺ was asked about his reaction to which he responded, "When this person began eating he forgot to pray *Bismillah*. Shaytan joined him in his food. But

no sooner did he remember to say *Bismillah*, then the accursed vomited everything he ate with the person."

(Mishkat al-Masabih)

When we begin to eat or drink something we should always remember to say *Bismillah*. It is the saying of Muhammad ﷺ that the accursed Shaytan joins in our food when we fail to recite it. And by praying it, the accursed cannot join in our eating and drinking. It has also been said in *Mishkat al-Masabih* that when a person enters there own home they should at that moment recite *Bismillah*. This is because it prevents Shaytan and his followers from staying in that house in the night, and from eating and drinking.

We learn from this valuable story that if we recite the Qur'an over food, like *Bismillah*, then the Shaytan cannot come near it. Shaytan is so afraid and scared of the Holy Qur'an that he stays away from food and drink on which the Qur'an is recited. And if he does consume that food and drink, by hearing the name of the Qur'an makes him vomit that food out.

• 48 •

Shaytan and a Girl

Sayyiduna Huzayfa ﷺ says that at the time of eating, nobody ate until the Messenger of Allah ﷺ began to eat.

One day we accompanied the Prophet of Allah to a dinner invitation. The food was brought to us and we waited for the Prophet to start. A small girl came along and made her way towards the food. As she put her hand forward the Prophet grabbed her hand and stopped her. A Bedoiun in that time also arrived and began to head for the food. And like before the Prophet of Allah ﷺ stopped him in his tracks. The Prophet of Allah ﷺ said, "Shaytan wishes that we begin to eat without saying *Bismillah* so that he can join us in the food. Hence the accursed came along with this girl and made her start in haste, but I managed to stop her. The accursed then came along with the Bedouin to eat, but I managed to stop him then as well." The Prophet of Allah ﷺ read *Bismillah* and he began to eat.

(Mishkat al-Masabih)

Shaytan is scared from the name of Allah, namely *Bismillah*. Whatever work or action begins with this name, the accursed can have no part to play in it. This is why Shaytan wishes that we do not pray it when we begin to do things such as eating. Hence Muslims should make every effort that when they eat and drink or do any well-intended action they say *Bismillah* at the start so that the accursed is not a party to that action.

We also learn that the noble Companions of the Prophet had the utmost respect and honour for him. This is shown in the fact that they did not begin to eat until their Master and Saviour ﷺ began to eat. Hence we too should have the utmost respect and honour for the Beloved of Allah ﷺ. This is because all our actions would come to nothing if we do not have this respect and honour for him.

Shaytan and Sayyiduna Umar

The Prophet of Allah ﷺ made a safe return from one of his battles when a woman came in the presence of his blessed presence. The woman told the Prophet of Allah ﷺ that she had made a vow that if he returned safely from the battle, she would sing with the duff in happiness of his safe return in front of him ﷺ. The Prophet of Allah ﷺ said to the lady that if that is your vow then keep it, otherwise do not. The lady said to the Prophet of Allah ﷺ that she intended to keep her vow so she began to play the duff and sing praises of the Prophet in front of him. The lady was singing as

Sayyiduna Abu Bakr Siddiq ﷺ appeared. The lady saw him and continued to sing. Sayyiduna Ali ﷺ also appeared and the lady continued to sing. The same occurred as Sayyiduna Uthman ﷺ made his presence felt. But when Sayyiduna Umar al-Khattab ﷺ appeared the lady stopped singing and hid the duff. The Prophet of Allah ﷺ saw the response of the lady and said to Sayyiduna Umar, "O Umar! This lady was playing the duff before you arrived, but once you arrived she stopped. O Umar! Shaytan is scared of you too."

(Mishkat al-Masabih)

Sayyiduna Umar ibn al-Khattab ﷺ is so awe-inspiring and fearsome and has so much dignity that the accursed Shaytan is scared of him. Whenever he hears his name he begins to tremble in fear. The lady was playing the duff in front of the Prophet of Allah ﷺ. Sayyiduna Abu Bakr Siddiq was there and so was Sayyiduna Uthman and Sayyiduna Ali ﷺ but the lady continued to play and sing. But when Sayyiduna Umar appeared she got frightened and stopped playing and singing.

The Hadith masters have made a very faith inspiring point with regards to this particular narration. They say that someone reading this Hadith may think that the status and honour of Sayyiduna Umar has been placed above that of the Holy Prophet. Because, they argue, the lady did not fear the Prophet as she played in front of him but did so when Sayyiduna Umar ؓ appeared. The answer to this is that if a man sits somewhere without a stick then a dog will not be fearful of them and in awe of that person if they did. If a man however has a stick in his hand then the dog's attitude changes and becomes fearful and vigilant to the extent that the dog may run away by seeing the stick. So can we say then that the stick carries greater awe and fear than the man because the dog did not fear the man did so with the stick? No! This is not the case. The stick is in actual fact shows the awe-inspiring nature and fearsomeness of the man. The awe of the stick really belongs to the person who carries it, because a stick by itself is nothing to be fearful of. Similarly the Prophet of Allah's stick in this case is Sayyiduna Umar ibn al-Khattab. While he was not there, the singing and playing continued. But once the awe and presence of Sayyiduna Umar ibn al-Khattab ﷺ came then the dog that is Shaytan fled in fear as the lady hid the duff. This awe-inspiring attribute belongs in this case to Sayyiduna Muhammad ﷺ but also to Sayyiduna Umar al-Khattab ﷺ .

We learn from this story, that the Prophet of Allah ﷺ is independent when it comes to implementing and interpreting the Shariah. He is allowed to interpret the Shariah as he sees fit and nobody can say anything against it. If he wishes, then women can play the duff in front him and sing. If the Prophet of Allah has given permission to it, who then is to stop her?

50

Shaytan and Money

Sayyiduna Ibn Abbas ﷺ narrates that when the first coin was minted the accursed Shaytan took it and gave it a kiss. He then put it in between his eyes and then on his navel and said, "By your means I will make people rebellious. And by you I will make people unbelievers. I am pleased at the fact that the children of Adam become happy at seeing you which makes them following me much easier."

(Talbis Iblis)

Shaytan's biggest trap against mankind is money. Many people have fell victim of the accursed Shaytan's plans and schemes. Bribery, deceit, usury, interest, smuggling and theft are all a result of the lure for money. This lure leads them to these crimes to the extent that people fall out of Islam. For the sake of money, people launder money, make false promises, statements and claims. They do not care as to what they are doing by deceiving others and more importantly themselves. The chase and lure of money destroys people's lives and futures. The reality is that money comes and money goes. All the hard work they strive to earn the money is wasted. Such people are described in the Qur'an as the losers of the world and the hereafter. Hence Muslims should be careful of this very powerful and potent trap and weapon of the accursed Shaytan. We Muslims should use money only within the realms of Shari'ah and treat it as such. But whoever leaves the advice and admonition of Islam in this respect will fall victim of this disease and will be destroyed in this world and in the hereafter.

Shaytan and Modern Times

A respected elder says that once he met the accursed Shaytan and started talking to him. Shaytan said to the man "Hazrat! What shall I tell you! There was a time when I use to mingle with the people and teach them bad things. But the situation is now the opposite. I go and meet the people and they are teaching me!"

(Talbis Iblis)

The tricksters, fraudsters, deceivers and liars of today's age are so evil in there ways that even Shaytan is surprised and astonished by their antics. The time has come where the accursed Shaytan is learning from men and not the other way round, which means that Shaytan has succeeded in deceiving people out of the Truth and will take them with him into the Hell fire.

Shaytan's Finger

A person once saw the accursed Shaytan about to lift his finger. The person said to Shaytan, "What are you about to do with this raised finger?" Shaytan said, "With this finger I do many things. People who quarrel and fight amongst themselves is a result of the movement of this finger." The person, astounded by what he heard, asked Shaytan how that could be. Shaytan in order to convince the person told him to join him in a short journey in which he would illustrate what he meant. Shaytan said, "This city in front of us I will destroy as a result of my finger. I will raise my finger only once and the whole city will be plunged into disorder, anarchy, bloodshed and savagery. Shaytan said these words and entered the city.

Shaytan made his way to the sweet stall where sweets

and delicacies were being made. Shaytan put some sugar in a hot pan and started making syrup out of it. The syrup began to boil as Shaytan said, "Look now at what my finger does to this City." Shaytan put his finger in the hot syrup and wiped it on a wall. "Just look at what happens," the accursed said.

A fly came along and sat on the syrup on the wall. More flies came and started eating the syrup. A lizard saw this swarm of flies and decided to attack and eat them. The owner of the sweet store had a cat. It saw the lizard and attacked it. Just as the cat was making its move, two soldiers walked passed the shop. The soldiers had with them their dog. The dog barked at the cat and attacked the cat. The cat tried to escape from the dog. In doing so she fell into the boiling syrup and died. The sweet shop owner saw what happened to its pet and started to attack the army dog. The soldiers in return attacked and beat up the sweet shop owner. The soldiers ended up killing the cat owner. The friends and relatives of the man found out what happened and attacked the two soldiers and killed them too. The army was made aware of what had happened to their patrolling soldiers and responded in a harsh and heavy manner. The army, in the desire of gaining revenge, set the whole city on a course of catastrophe as the inhabitants were embroiled in fighting and bloodshed. Shaytan, watching the city fall apart, said to the person "did you see the wonders of my finger? All I did was lift my finger once and the people started to kill each other!"

(Mughni al-Wa'izin)

Every Fitna, *Fasaad* and trouble is initiated and stimulated by the accursed Shaytan. The accursed has his finger over his enemies. Today, the pot in which the West has made their "syrup" has the finger of Shaytan in it. Shaytan has put his finger in this pot, made by Europe and America, and has smeared it all over the world. We now know the cause of Fitna and *Fasaad* across the whole world and whose finger is behind it. On this syrup, the flies of indecency and deceit are licking away at this syrup. In some corner the lizard called fashion appears. The ill-looking cat appears and makes its mark. The dog called seduction pounces. From here, the fighting, dissent, killing and bloodshed begins. Shaytan as a result becomes happy that his finger has done its work.

• 53 •

Shaytan and the Conquest of Iran

To the west of Iran there is a land called Kurdistan (which is now part of Iraq). In ancient times this place was called Aria. The leader of that area, Zahak, invaded Iran. A very big and hard fought battle took place. But Jamshed was defeated and killed. Zahak conquered Iran. It is said about him that he would

roast men in fire, put a sprinkle of salt on them and eat them.

Shaytan in the appearance of a man went to Zahak. Shaytan took with him a chicken dish with salt and spices garnished in butter and offered it to him. Zahak was pleased to receive it and ate it. He said to the stranger, "Ask whatever you want and I will grant it to you". Shaytan with great respect said to Zahak that it was his wish that he could kiss him between his two shoulder blades. Zahak gave permission for this request. Shaytan went behind him to kiss but turned into two snakes instead and started biting him. Zahak screamed in pain and called for a surgeon to remove the snake. But the snakes reappeared. In that time, Shaytan appeared again as a different person this time as a herbalist and said, "O King! The snake will not go away by cutting it. All you need to do is to eat a human every day and the snake will not harm you."

After that Zahak did as he was told and killed his

subjects so that he could feel ease. He killed two men to feed the snakes every day. In the King's palace lived a blacksmith. His name was Ka'wah. He had twelve sons. In no time at all they were the target of the snakes. Ka'wah by now had enough of this fiasco which was engulfing the land and felt a sense of revenge and anger as he went about ending this murder and bloodshed. He got his bellows, which he used as a blacksmith, and made a flag. He called upon all the oppressed victims of the king to unite under him so that they could challenge his tyrannical rule. He led these people against Zahak and toppled him from power, as the dictator was killed. The people of this land were finally given respite from this tyranny and oppression.

(Akhbaar Mashriq Lahore, Jashne Iran No. 15, October 1970)

Shaytan changes his appearance into that of a human being in order to con and deceive mankind. This is why the great Maulana Rumi said:

'At times Shaytan's presence is in human shape,
therefore do not give your hand into every hand'

We learn from this valuable story that Shaytan uses very tasty and tempting foods to trap and entice people. He uses such tempting things to trap them within his evil and disastrous plans. We also learn that on the face of it, the accursed can appear to be a being of goodwill and honesty. But in this "love" of his is his evilness as this love turns into hatred and destruction, as the story clearly illustrates. The accursed Shaytan also appears in one moment as a person who gives pain and then the next moment as a doctor or physician. In other words Shaytan changes his approach and appearance which suits the circumstances he works in which inevitably leads to catastrophe. Whoever gets caught in his evil web is sure to be destroyed. Such is the nature of Shaytan's work that others get caught up in it as well.

54

A Tailor

Maulana Rumi narrated a story of a tailor who was known for cutting pieces of cloth from people's clothes and keeping it for himself. Whoever went and gave him cloth to sow, the tailor would take some for himself and the customer would not know about it. A soldier learnt about this man and wanted to test the tailor and see whether he could get away from him or not. The soldier thought that he would be able to keep an eye on him so that the tailor would not be able to take anything.

Hence the soldier took some cloth to the tailor for a coat to be made out of it. As he gave the cloth to him the soldier said "Tailor! I have heard much about you. I have heard that you steal people's cloth without them knowing about it. But I have come to tell you that I am not like ordinary people and I have come here to keep a real look out on you to make sure that you do not cheat me out of my cloth and coat. Cut this cloth in front of me and let us see if you succeed in taking cloth from me!"

The tailor was a very clever and sharp man. He said to him, "Come and sit down! Which fool has put you into doubt about my profession and me? I have done tailoring all my life and I have not stolen a single yard of cloth. I feel that such deception is unacceptable. Anyhow, it may be that I could give a silly person a run for their money. But with a wise and intelligent man like you I could never deceive you!"

The soldier said to the tailor, "Fine. Go ahead and cut my coat and let us see if you do deceive me." The tailor took the cloth and his scissors and began to cut out the cloth for the soldier's coat. The soldier was looking intensely at the tailor's every move to make sure he did not try anything suspicious. The tailor burst out laughing as he told the soldier that he was a very witty and comical man. The tailor began to tell the soldier jokes. The tailor told him joke after joke as he was cutting the cloth. The tailor told the soldier one particular joke. He laughed so much that the soldier looked down at the floor and held his stomach. The tailor grasped this opportunity and cut a piece of cloth for himself and stashed it away without the soldier noticing. The soldier was now so engrossed in the witty tailor's jokes that he asked him to tell him more jokes. The tailor did as requested and told another brilliant joke. And like before, the soldier was in stitches as he laughed so much at the jokes that his face was on the floor in laughter. Like before the tailor took some more cloth off the soldier's coat. The soldier asked again for the comical tailor to tell him a joke when the tailor said to him, "I could tell you a third joke, but if I did, I would have to take some more cloth off you coat which then would be too tight for you!"

This story narrated by the great Maulana Rumi ﷺ shows in clear terms that the example of the soldier in this story is like that of a heedless and thoughtless human being against the tricks and deceit of Shaytan. It is like a man who thinks he is very good and pious and cannot be deceived. But Shaytan comes along with his scissors and cuts away at this man's character to the extent that he makes him feel uncomfortable. Shaytan with these scissors is looking at every opportunity to cut away at people's *Iman* and good actions so that there is nothing left for them to carry forward in the *Akhirah*. The heedless man thinks he can compete against the tricky Shaytan, but the Devil entices such people into such stories, jokes and schemes that the heedless person is caught inside worldly desires and thoughts. This sort of trap laid down by the accursed makes it much easier for him to cut away at people's faith. In no time at all the heedless man is left with nothing at all as all his work and efforts have been taken away from him right in front of his own eyes.

55

Thief

The following story is from *Mathnawi Sharif* by Maulana Rumi ﷺ.

A person brought a sheep from a market and was making his way back home. The man had a long rope. He tied one end of it round the neck of the sheep and held the other end in his hand. The long rope meant that the sheep trailed its new owner by quite a distance. A thief took this opportunist moment to steal the sheep. He carefully made his way in between the man and the sheep and cut the rope in between. The thief took the sheep away, as the owner did not realise what was happening. The man went along, when he turned round to see that the rope he was pulling along had no sheep at the end of it. The man ran back to where he had come from and went in search of his sheep. While he was searching for his sheep, he came across a man at a well who was crying and looked very worried. The man asked him why he was crying. The person said that he had dropped his wallet which contained one hundred rupees. He asked if he would be kind enough to go to the bottom of the well and fish it out for him. If he did so, then he would reward him with fifty rupees. The man who just lost his sheep, thought of this as an opportunity to earn a quick financial reward, which would allow him to buy another sheep. The man quickly agreed to the proposition made by the man at the well and made his way down the well with the aid of the rope he had with him. The man took his clothes off and made his way down the well. When he got down there he looked long and hard for the wallet but could not find it. Disappointed at not finding it, the man made his way back up. When he reached the summit he found that the worried man was nowhere to be seen and his clothes had been taken as well. This unfortunate man was left naked and robbed of his sheep and rope.

The man who made the excuse at the well was in actual fact the same person who stole the man's sheep in the first place. Not only did he steal his sheep, but also his rope, his clothes and his dignity.

(Mathnawi Sharif)

The thief who stole the man's belongings is a reflection of the character and nature of our enemy Shaytan. The accursed makes us heedless of our religion and faith and comes from behind us to cut the rope of our faith without us knowing about it. This heedless man, in pursuit of worldly greed, enters the well of hopes and desires. The man enters this deep and dark well of worldly desires and hopes, which makes his living futile. The end result is that this person is made naked and is robbed of all dignity and honour. Shaytan has made this well attractive to all people across the world with new hopes and desires. Immoral societies which are full of such evil and destructive things make humans devoid of dignity and honour by taking away their clothes of humanity and Islam. May Allah protect us from the vices of the world, Ameen.

56

A Swindler

One day a solicitor having had a bath in his home forgot to put his watch back on. He went to court without realising it. On the way to work a friend of his asked the time. The solicitor looked at his wrist to see that he forgot to wear his watch. He apologised to his friend. It just so happened that a swindler heard this comment and thought about taking the watch. The swindler asked people about the solicitor and managed to find out where he lived. On the way to the solicitor's home, he brought a live chicken. The swindler reached the house of the door and called out. An old woman responded and asked who it was. The swindler said that he had brought a chicken on behalf of the solicitor. And that he was asked to collect his watch, which was left in the bathroom. The old lady went to the bathroom to see the watch there. She took it and gave it to the swindler and took the chicken off him. The swindler succeeded in his aim and went away with the watch.

In the evening, the solicitor came back home from court. His wife asked him whether or not he got his watch or not. The solicitor in a state of shock said, "Watch? Sent by whom?" His wife told him that he himself had sent a man with a chicken and a message to bring the watch to him from the bathroom. The solicitor surprised by what was said showed no knowledge of what had happened just as the other members of the household were.

The next day, after the solicitor had gone to work, the swindler appeared again outside the house of the solicitor. He said to the lady, "The thief has been found. Please hand over the chicken as it is going to be used as evidence in the court". The old lady was happy to hear that the thief was court and handed over the chicken to the stranger. Evening came and the wife asked her husband, "Have you got the watch?" The husband said he hadn't. The wife scolded him and asked why he then asked for the chicken to be given into the court for evidence (in the trial). The solicitor was confounded as to what had happened. But there was nothing that he could do.

(Taybah Monthly, March 1963)

The watch swindler is an example of how the accursed Shaytan operates. The swindler used the chicken to entice the lady to give the watch for the chicken, but also took the chicken back the next day. The swindler took everything while the lady and solicitor had nothing. Like this, Shaytan lures us in to worldly desires and wishes and buys the clock of our faith in exchange. Shaytan like the swindler robs us not once but twice, thus making the humiliation complete. People who fall for such tricks are left nothing in the *Dunya* or in the *Akhira*. Such misfortunate people are to be avoided at all times.

57

Two Faced

A couple loved each other very much. An envious person did not like this beautiful relationship. They decided to pretend to be a household servant and started working there with the aim of destroying their relationship. The envious person worked hard around the house in order to impress. After a few days, the envious person went to the shop where the husband worked and said to him, "What I saw today at the house really made me angry. Your wife was with a strange man. I secretly listened in to their conversation and I learnt that they intend to live together. Your wife was saying that she was going to get you killed so that the way is made for them to live together." The husband heard this and became very scared. He began to have serious doubts about the wife he loved so much.

The envious servant reached home and started another false rumour to the woman of the house. The envious person told the woman that her husband was establishing illegal relations with another woman. This is why he is acting very strange. After a few days, the wife noticed the change in attitude from her husband and began to feel that the servant was right in what they were saying.

A few days had passed when the servant suggested to the wife that she should cut a few hairs off the beard of her husband, so that an amulet could be made by a Shaykh, so that their love could be rekindled. The wife, desperate to re-establish their relationship, agreed. The envious person gave the woman a razor blade. The wife was told to use that as her husband slept that night.

The envious person then went to the husband and said, "I would be careful tonight if I were you. Your wife will have a razor blade in her hand and she will try and slit your throat and kill you."

That evening, the husband reluctantly came home and went to rest on the bed. He felt tired but could not sleep because of what the servant said to him. His eyes were closed but he was not asleep.

Half the night had passed. The wife seeing her husband with his eyes closed thought that he had gone to sleep. She got and got hold of the razor as she went to cut some hairs out of his beard. As she approached him, the husband sensed something was about to happen. He got up took the blade of her and killed her there and then.

The next morning, the relatives and friends of the woman learnt what had happened and turned against him and killed him. The house that was a home to a loving couple turned to blood as a result of envy and suspicion.

(Taybah Monthly, August issue 1960)

The case of the envious servant is an example just like that of Shaytan. Blood boils when they see love and affection between husband and wife, brother and sister, mother and daughter, father and son and between elders and youngsters. They wish to destroy that pure relationship at all costs even if it means the spilling of innocent blood. The accursed Shaytan makes up small talk and blows it out of all proportions. This results in serious doubts amongst people causing doubt and then friction and dissension amongst people. This friction and dissension leads to hate and anger and not to love and affection.

• 58 •

In the Dark

A man from the tribe of Bani Aqeel came to steal a horse. He went about finding a way of stealing one when he entered a house. The house he entered was pitch black. He noticed that the owner of the house and his wife were eating dinner. The thief was hungry and joined in. As the thief extended his hand to eat the husband touched his hand and grabbed it. What the thief did was to grab the hand of the woman. The wife said to the husband, "Why are you holding my hand?" The husband thinking that he had grabbed his wife's hand let go. They all started to eat. After a while the wife touched the hand of the thief and grabbed it. Again realising the situation, the thief then grabbed the hand of the husband. The wife let go of the thief's hand and the thief did the same with the husband. They completed the dinner and went to sleep. The thief ate to the full and stole the horse he wanted.

(Kitab al-Azkiya)

The actions of the horse thief are just like that of the Devil. Just as the thief benefited from entering the house and took what he wanted, Shaytan also enters our lives and makes new ways and schemes of robbing us of our dignity and honour. Shaytan has his hands over women and men and deceives them both. Furthermore they do not realise that they are being conned. Shaytan in this manner not only robs us of the world but also of the Hereafter. And as with most people, we do not realise what happens until it is too late. May Allah protect us from being 'in the dark' with the Devil, Ameen.

• 59 •

Tricky Old Woman

In America, an old lady with a walking stick was walking along when she pounced on a young man. She started to hug him and kiss him and said, "O my God! Your face looks just like that of my son who is no more." The surprised young man took it to heart about the old lady's feelings and comforted her. The old lady then separated from him wiped her tears, apologised and went her own way. The young man turned the

street corner and went about his own business. But when he put his hands in his pockets, his wallet had gone missing.

(*Taybah Monthly, December 1958*)

This old tricky and deceitful woman is an exact example of how the accursed Shaytan works. There are people who recite to us Qur'an and Hadith and appear to be very good and warm-hearted and jovial. They have sweet voices and appear to be innocent in their work, but the reality is that they come and steal our *Iman* and *Aqidah* from us just like the young man lost his wallet. May Allah protect us from these tricky and deceitful people and from Shaytan – Ameen.

60

Shaytan and Azan

The Prophet of Allah ﷺ said:

"Shaytan upon hearing the Azan (call to Prayer) flees
as far as a place called Ruhaa"

(Mishkat al-Masabih)

Where is Ruhaa? Ruhaa is a place thirty-six miles away
from Madinah al Munawwara.

Allah rejected Shaytan for failing to do prostration to
Adam ﷺ. Prostration (*Sajda*) is the pinnacle of Prayer
and the Azan calls the Believers towards it. It is for this
reason that Shaytan runs away so far at hearing these
holy words five times a day. We learn from this that those
people who do not respond to the Muezzin and flee from
the mosques, these people are like the accursed Shaytan.

O Muslims! Don't flee when you hear the Azan. But instead flock towards the mosque and do *Sajda* to your Creator as He has ordered you to. To flee is the way of Shaytan. To respond to the Azan is the way of the Muslim.

I would like to ask a serious question to those people that do not pray in response to the Azan. Before the creation of Pakistan in 1947, Muslims lived with Hindus and Sikhs. When the Azan took place, no Hindu or Sikh would respond to the Azan and come to the mosque. If you were to say to them "The Azan has happened, why haven't you gone to the mosque", they would reply that the Azan is for Muslims, not for Hindus or Sikhs. Their response would be absolutely correct. But since the creation of a Muslim homeland, few Hindus or Sikhs live with us. So tell me this, when the Azan happens and people still do not come to the mosque for Prayer, what do those people say about themselves? Do these people think that the call to Prayer is not for them? If they think this then what do they think themselves to be? And if they do not feel like that then why do they not pray? This is a serious question that needs answering.

61

Shaytan's Four Acts of Disbelief (*Kufr*)

Allama Safoori ﷺ in his work *Nuzahatul Majaalis* states four acts of *Kufr* which Shaytan the accursed committed, resulting in his rejection.

1. The accursed attributed *Zulm* to the Holy and Pure qualities of Allah Almighty by saying: "I am better than him because you have made me out of fire while you have created him out of dust."

The accursed was saying that he was better than Adam ﷺ. And that he was being asked to bow down to something inferior. He was attributing *Zulm* to Allah and to do this is *Kufr*.

2. Shaytan looked at a chosen Prophet with contempt and defiance. To do this to any prophet of Allah is *Kufr*.

3. Shaytan went against the consensus of the majority, namely the angels. All the angels went into *Sajda* except Iblis. To defy the consensus of the majority is *Kufr*.

4. When asked by Allah Almighty why he rejected His order, he presented his false philosophy that fire was better than dust. His presentation of this false philosophy in the court of Allah is *Kufr*.

(Nuzahatul Majaalis)

We should make strenuous efforts to avoid these acts and traits of the accursed Shaytan. We should never even contemplate uttering anything wrong or unjust against

Allah Almighty. Some people out of sheer ignorance and stupidity say, "God's injustice" (Allah forbid!) these words should never be uttered. Such association with the Almighty is the way of Shaytan. We should regard every action of the Almighty and wise and perfect. Indeed He knows what we know not.

Shaytan's second act of *Kufr* is an act that all Muslims should try and avoid. That is to regard Allah's prophets in contempt and disdain. Allah immensely dislikes it when His Prophets are treated with or regarded with contempt and disrespect. Such actions lead to *Kufr*. Shaytan had worshipped Allah for countless years but his worship came to naught as he rejected Allah's command. His thousands of years of worship and belief in Tawhid came to nothing. We learn then that to protect our faith we need to have belief in Tawhid but also in Prophethood. Hence Muslims should have the utmost respect for the prophets and no more so for the leader of all the Prophets Sayyiduna Muhammad ﷺ. We should never contemplate or utter any words that show contempt and disdain at the Prophet. Hence we should not say that he is human like us. Or that he eats like us or drinks like us or sleeps like us (*Ma'azallah*). To attribute such sayings to Allah's chosen men of guidance and salvation is totally wrong. Such contempt and disdain is the way of Shaytan.

Shaytan's third act of *Kufr* was to go against the overwhelming consensus of the majority. All the angels bowed down except him, who stood alone in defiance. The angels accepted the truth while Shaytan rejected it.

It is Allah's favour upon us that the Ahl al-Sunna wa'l Jama'at as He has wished, is the biggest group and majority group amongst the Muslims today. We must strive to stay with the largest group and not to deviate and join or associate ourselves with any other groups. The Prophet of Allah ﷺ has advised us by saying, "Follow the biggest group (i.e. the majority)."

Shaytan's fourth act of *Kufr* was to present his "logic" in front of Allah. The accursed presented his false philosophy that fire is better than dust and hence why he was not going to bow down to Adam ﷺ. We must avoid this habit of asking why. Allah Almighty has told us to pray Salah, offer Zakah, fast and to offer the Hajj. Every single Muslim, male and female, should surrender to these orders and carry them out without objection. We should not start making up false philosophies by saying "why should I pray?" or "why must I fast?" Such thoughts make the accursed happy as we are following his "logic". But the real logic is to obey without question the orders of Allah. We should strive to avoid the path of the Devil and instead adopt the character traits of the angels and bow down and surrender immediately and without question.

The Philosopher's
Three Questions

A philosopher announced that he had three questions that he wanted answering by a scholar. If a scholar gave him a satisfactory response he would believe them. His three questions were as follows.

1. When nobody has seen Allah, why then do we say in the *Kalima* "I bear witness that there is no deity but Him?"

2. What happens is Allah's will. So why are humans guilty for their mistakes if they are not doing it but Allah?

3. Shaytan according to the Qur'an is made of fire.

The Hell fire is waiting for him after the day of Judgement. How can the Hell fire harm him when he is made of fire? Fire cannot hurt fire, so what is the point in the punishment?

A few days had passed since he had announced his questions in public for answering. As a result, he began to mock the scholars of religion for failing to respond to his questions.

One day, outside the city, he passed by a field. There he saw an old and respected man. Next to him was a big clay pot. The old man called the philosopher over and said to him that he had heard that he had posed some questions which nobody till now could answer. The philosopher replied in the affirmative.

Old man: Tell me the questions, maybe I will be able to answer them.
The philosopher repeated his three questions to the old man.

Old man: I can give you the three answers.

Philosopher: Go ahead.

The old man got hold of his clay pot and smashed it against the philosopher's head. The philosopher started to scream in pain at the old man asking him why he had smashed his clay pot against his head.

Old man: I have just given the answers to your three questions.

Philosopher: Are you joking with me, I will take you to court.

The philosopher went to court and petitioned the judge. The judge summoned the old man who stood in court with the philosopher.

Judge: Did you hit this man on the head with a clay pot?

Old man: Yes, I did.

Judge: Why?

The old man: I was giving him the answers to his three philosophical questions.

Judge: How did you manage that?

Old man: The man asked me how it was possible to

give witness to Allah when we haven't see Him.

The man then turned towards the philosopher.

What happened with the clay pot?

Philosopher: You hit me on the head with it.

Old man: And does your head hurt?

Philosopher: Yes, my head hurts a lot.

Old man: Who will give witness to this claim?

Philosopher: I do.

Old man: You testify yourself that you were hurt? This pain you talk about - you haven't seen it, so how can you give testimony of it to others?

Philosopher: I haven't seen the pain, but I can feel it.

Old man: Just as you can feel the pain and not see it, we bear witness to the Almighty Allah, without seeing Him, because we feel His mercy and favours upon us.

Philosopher: I see. I understand the first question now.

The old man then moved on to the second question.

Old man: You talked about how Allah wills, and yet humans are held to account. According to your logic Allah hit the pot on your head not me. So why am I standing here in court?

Philosopher: The second question has been resolved. I now understand it. But my third question remains.

Old man Ah! But that also has been answered.

Philosopher: How is that?

Old man: You said, if Shaytan is made of fire and the Hell is full of fire, then what harm is there upon him?

Philosopher: That is right.

Old man: What is your skull made out of?

Philosopher: Bone (i.e. soil, clay).

Old man: And what is the pot made out of?

Philosopher: Clay

Old man: And did you get hurt by it?

Philosopher: Yes I did.

Old man: As just as your clay skull got hurt by a clay pot, Shaytan will get hurt immensely in the Hell fire.

Philosopher Very good. My questions have been answered.

63

Shaytan's Crying

The Prophet of Allah ﷺ him said:

"The tears of a sinful Muslim extinguish
the wrath of Allah."

Allama Safoori ﷺ has commented that IF it was said
that Shaytan cried a lot after his sin, then why didn't
his tears extinguish Allah's wrath upon him?" The
answer to this lies in the Hadith narrated above. The
words of the Hadith say "tears of sinners" not "tears
of non-Muslims". The tears of the non-believer are
like poison, while the tears of the sinful Muslim are
remedial.

(Nuzahatul Majaalis)

We learn from this Hadith that salvation comes only from

having *Iman* (faith). If you have *Iman* then good deeds and actions will be beneficial. If for some reason sins and mistakes are committed, then crying and repenting for it will also be beneficial as it helps extinguish Allah's wrath. In other words, a sinful Muslim whose *Iman* is correct and sheds tears in fear of Allah will enjoy the benefits of Allah's mercy. But for the non-believer, his tears will be to no use because he will not have faith to rely upon. This can be explained further with the following example. If you sow a seed, and then water it, then the seed will grow. But if there is no seed in the soil, then it does not matter how much water you put on, a seed will not grow into something. The Hadith of our Beloved Prophet ﷺ is for the Muslim who truly believes, not for those who do not. Tears of regret to Allah are beneficial to the Muslim, not to the non-Muslim.

Heaven and Heart

Allah Almighty says "O believer! My Jannat is your home and your heart is Mine. I will not allow Shaytan, your enemy, into your home and nor can he enter. So why do you not stop Shaytan entering your heart, which is my home. If you allow Shaytan inside your heart, (namely my home) then this is unjust upon Me. Fill your heart with My Remembrance (*Zikr*). Don't let the enemy in.

Do not ever leave the heart void of My remembrance
Owls live there where nobody lives

Owls reside in empty and derelict areas. If you do not fill your heart (i.e. my home) with My Remembrance, the accursed Shaytan will start residing in there. Shame! Today's "hearts" are becoming void of Allah's *Zikr*, and are being populated with Shaytan's ways instead.

The Non-Worshipper

A poet wrote:

Giya Shaytan mara ik sajdeh ki na karneh seh
Agar laakho baras sajdeh meh sar mara hota

Shaytan was rejected for not doing one prostration
Despite having surrendered his
head for thousands of years

Shaytan worshipped for thousands of years. But because
he failed to perform one *Sajda* - which was to Adam and
not even Allah - he was rejected and humiliated.

So think about the order Allah has given to perform Salah five times a day, which we sometimes fail to fulfil. Such a person is committing a worse act than Shaytan. Shaytan denied only one *Sajda*, while you deny hundred, thousands of them.

· 66 ·

A Message To Those Who Do Not Fast

A poet once wrote:

What laughter I get seeing the actions of mankind
They act bad themselves and then curse Shaytan!

Humans get up to such actions and misdeeds that Shaytan himself is dumbfounded by it. Humans

do wrong themselves, and then use Shaytan as a scapegoat and blame the accursed instead.

A scholar once made a speech in which he said that on the Day of Judgement, Allah will call upon those people who missed the Salah. The non-worshipper will say that Shaytan distracted him and stopped him from praying. It may be possible that Allah would forgive that person.

But if some person who deliberately misses the fast was summoned by Allah on the Day of Judgement, and tried to present the same excuse, then the following would happen. Shaytan upon hearing this excuse would complain to Allah and say, "O Allah according to your Prophet ﷺ, the Shaytan is chained and locked away in the month of Ramadan. So how is it possible that I stopped them from fasting?" Shaytan will say, "O Allah! This person is guilty, this is not my doing! This person broke and missed the fast himself, not me". As a result of this satanic intervention, the person who misses the fasts deliberately will have no excuse whatsoever.

The Prevention of Giving Charity

Ibn Jawzi reports in *Talbis Iblis* that Shaytan tries and traps humans with nice things. When Shaytan gets frustrated, he lies down in people's wealth and stops people from giving charity. We learn from this that those who are charitable in the way of Allah are outside the influence of the accursed. And those who are not charitable and criticise others for being charitable for the sake of Allah are caught in Shaytan's web. Shaytan is lying down in their wealth.

False Dervishes and Hermits

Imam Ibn Jawzi in *Talbis Iblis* made the following observation. One of Shaytan's many deceptions is that he criticises the general Muslim public (laymen) for "falling for" and believing in artificial mystics and dervishes who are separated from worldly thoughts. Not only that but they give pre-eminence to the *Ulama*. If these people were to see a Sufi dressed in cotton clothing, then immediately they fell for them and say that there is no one better than them. Shaytan argues that these people are cut off from the *Dunya*. They do not marry, do not dress well, eat well, nor live comfortably and decent lives.

All these type of comments are part of Shaytan's trap and web of deceit and misinformation. It is an attack and insult of the Shariah of Muhammad ﷺ to say that the people on the true Sufi path give pre-eminence of their own ways to that of the Prophet of Allah, and that these people have given authority to themselves.

It is a massive favour of Allah that such deceitful people were not around in the time of the Prophet ﷺ. Because if they were then they would have objected to him of marrying and having a family, and eating sweets and enjoyable foods (on some occasions). If they were around then they would have lost all confidence and faith in the Prophet of Allah ﷺ.